The Bible and the Making of Modern India

Endorsements

Vishal has read the pulse of our time and tapped into a profound reality that illuminates the steepest of sceptics.

Modern India was and continues to be forged in the image of the Christian Bible. Many have tried to reverse the flow of Judeo-Christian thinking across the Indian subcontinent, but God's word relentlessly persists and persuades even against the gale force winds of charismatic leaders who wish to see it diminish and disappear.

When India gained its independence from British rule, well-furnished minds like Justice Krishna Iyer were very precise on the path India would need to take if it were to survive as an Independent nation. In his formidable style, Mr Iyer wrote, *'Not the Potomac but the Thames fertilises the flow of the Yamuna..."*

The Westminster model of governance is filled with Biblical dynamics, which is why it is no surprise that when Dr. Manmohan Singh received his honorary degree from Oxford, England, he said quite clearly, *"we did not entirely reject the British claim to good governance. We merely asserted our natural right to self-governance.'*

Vishal's masterpiece here will reveal where the former Prime Minister of India acquired the concept of 'self-governance' and why there is an intense desire to nurture it, as Mr. Iyer noted quite intriguingly during India's birth years.

— **Rahil Patel,**
Former Hindu monk, author of *Found By Love*,
Speaker & tutor at The Oxford Centre for Christian Apologetics

The thesis presented by Vishal Mangalwadi in this book is simple yet startling. The Bible is not merely a religious book that guides individual seekers in their personal quest to connect with God. It is a roadmap for entire communities, societies, and nations that are honestly grappling with questions of lasting peace and non-discriminatory prosperity, and, as in the case of India, a genuine unity in diversity.

— **Professor Ashish Alexander,**

Dean, School of Humanities and Social Sciences, Sam Higginbottom University of Agriculture, Technology and Sciences

This book offers a meticulously researched historical account of the events of the last 300 years that shaped the formation of India. The facts are presented as they unfolded—unembellished, unvarnished, and deeply thought-provoking. It challenges conventional narratives and dismantles stereotypes, urging readers to confront truths that many often overlook. This is a book for those unafraid to follow the truth wherever it leads. But if you're content with your assumptions and prefer not to have your worldview challenged, consider passing it on to a friend with a more open mind.

— **Dr. Vinod Shah**
Pediatric surgeon, Christian Medical College, Vellore, former CEO of Emmanuel Hospital Association, former CEO of the International Christian Medical and Dental Association

Vishal Mangalwadi's *The Bible and the Making of Modern India* is a profound work that delves deeply into the biblical, philosophical, and historical foundations shaping modern India. With remarkable insight, Mangalwadi demonstrates how the Bible played a crucial role in the country's development. This book is a must-read for anyone seeking to understand the significant influence of biblical principles in the formation of modern India. I highly recommend it for its depth, clarity, and compelling exploration of India's intellectual and cultural roots.

— **Pankaj Parmar,**
Trinitarian Metanarrative thinker and mentor, Founder, Satya Today Apologetics

Dr. Mangalwadi's book, '*The Bible and the Making of Modern India*', is a fascinating and eye-opening read that unfolds the forgotten and untold history of India. By shedding light on the significant contributions of unsung heroes who worked tirelessly for the country's progress over the past two centuries, this book is a must-read for anyone interested in Indian history, culture, and the impact of the Bible on India's progress.

— **Priya Aristotle,**
Advocate, Supreme Court of India

Myth and Truth are two powerful narratives engaged in a bitter fight in India today. While Myth goes to all lengths and breadth of gymnastics to prove its worthiness, Truth stands still and tall, with its substance unadulterated for anyone to explore. Dr. Vishal's ability to collate facts and figures and put them in perspective is just too marvelous to bring out this powerful book for anyone to know the truth about the making of modern India.

Just read this book and you will indeed come to the conclusion on your own that it is the Bible, along with the walking Bibles, as in missionaries, that built modern India brick by brick. They laid a solid foundation for a strong democracy, cementing all the virtues of unity in diversity and paving the way for a nation to embrace freedom, equality and fraternity for its citizens. I am sure you will be compelled to read the other books penned by Dr. Vishal.

— **Kiran Ajit Kujur,**
Director, Orion Greenventures

Some of the most popular foods in India—biryani, samosa, jalebi, gulab jamun, and tea—are not native to India but originate from the Middle East and China. Similarly, almost all the ideals on which modern India is based, such as democracy, liberty, justice, education, and scientific temper, are not native to India but to the West. They are as foreign as samosa, tea, and jalebi. But, over the course of two centuries or so, these ideals have become so ingrained in society that they now appear to be from India, much like tea and samosa.

Dr. Mangalwadi separates your native roti ideas from your grand biryani and traces their origins, explaining how they came to India in this wholesome book.

— **Prasanth David,**
Former Silicon Valley entrepreneur

Dedicated to the
Union of Evangelical Students of India (UESI)
who taught me to make reverential Bible-reading a daily habit

The Bible and the Making of Modern India
(Revised Edition)

Copyright © 2025 by Vishal Mangalwadi

Published by

Sought After Media

www.SoughtAfterMedia.com

Email: manager@SoughtAfterMedia.com

1077 N. Willow Ave

Ste 105 PMB 1010

Clovis, CA 93611-4411

USA

Distributed by

www.Triaze.com

Email: triaze@ruahtech.com.au

Most Scripture quotations are taken from The Holy Bible, New International Version, NIV, Copyright © 1973, 1978, 1984, 2011 by Biblica Inc. Used with permission. All rights reserved worldwide.

ISBN 979-8-9887831-8-3

"The worst [thing] about the new Constitution of Bharat [India] is that there is nothing Bharatiya (Indian) about it."

- Vinayak Damodar Savarkar,
Hindutva ideologue, President of Hindu Mahasabha, the forerunner of Jan Sangh & Bharatiya Janata Party (BJP)
"Women in Manusmriti" in *Sarvarkar Samagra, Collection of Savarkar's Writings in Hindi* Prabhat, New Delhi

Contents

Foreword	XV
Preface	XIX
Introduction	XXIII
1. The Bible and the Idea of India	1
2. The Bible and India's Renaissance	13
3. The Bible Explodes Indian Fatalism	27
4. The Bible Reformed the British Raj	39
5. The Bible and Women's Liberation	49
6. The Bible and India's Green Revolution	69
7. The Bible, Not Britain, Modernised India	83
8. The Bible and India's Independence	103
9. The Bible and the Soul of Modern India	117
10. The Bible and India's Future	127
Other books by the author	143
Acknowledgements	188

Foreword

Rev. Dr. Richard Howell

In celebration of Dr. Vishal Mangalwadi's 75th birthday, *The Bible and the Making of Modern India* highlights the remarkable influence of biblical principles on India's transformation into a sovereign, inclusive, and progressive nation. Through this work, Mangalwadi offers a profound exploration of how the Bible catalysed social, cultural, and intellectual revolutions in India, presenting a fresh perspective on its historical significance.

India's pre-modern society was marked by caste divisions, fatalistic worldviews, and rigid hierarchies that often stifled progress. Mangalwadi demonstrates how biblical principles introduced new ideas of human dignity, equality, and moral responsibility, disrupting these entrenched systems. Concepts such as nationhood and sovereignty, previously alien to Indian society, emerged as transformative forces inspired by the Bible. These principles spurred reforms that tackled issues like child marriage and widow-burning (sati), replacing pessimistic fatalism with hope and a belief in human potential.

A cornerstone of the Bible's impact in India was its role in education and language development. Missionaries like William Carey translated regional dialects into written languages, democratising knowledge and making it accessible to the masses. This linguistic revolution empowered marginalised communities and fostered intellectual and cultural growth nationwide. Mangalwadi emphasises how the Bible encouraged the education of women and the underprivileged, dismantling exclusivity in traditional systems. Influential reformers such as Raja Ram Mohan Roy (1772–1833) and Pandita Ramabai (1858–1922), inspired by the Bible, became champions of social and cultural transformation.

The Bible's emphasis on justice and human rights laid the groundwork for India's modern legal and administrative systems. Mangalwadi highlights how missionaries and reformers, driven by biblical teachings, often stood against colonial exploitation. They advocated for justice, liberty, and the uplift of the oppressed, contributing to developing the

Indian Penal Code and ethical governance structures. By championing the rights of the downtrodden, these reformers made enduring contributions to India's legal and political landscape.

The Bible also played a critical role in fostering a sense of national identity. Its unifying vision united India's fragmented communities, inspiring nationalist poetry, movements, and intellectual renaissances. While figures like Mahatma Gandhi (1869–1948) and B.R. Ambedkar (1891–1956) did not accept the Bible as God's word, their missions were influenced by the Bible's values of justice and equality. This foundation offered a framework for socio-political transformation and cultural integration.

Mangalwadi's work also challenges reductive historical interpretations of colonialism. By distinguishing the Bible's influence from the exploitative motives of imperial powers, he sheds light on the missionaries and reformers who opposed colonial authorities to advocate for justice and the welfare of the oppressed. This nuanced perspective underscores the Bible's role as a force for positive change, countering simplistic narratives of colonial history.

At a time when India's identity and values are under intense scrutiny, *The Bible and the Making of Modern India* serve as a vital reminder of the diverse influences that have shaped the nation. Mangalwadi invites readers to reflect on how biblical principles of truth, justice, and compassion remain relevant to addressing today's challenges. His book bridges history and contemporary issues, offering a historical analysis and a vision for India's future rooted in ethical governance and inclusive progress.

The Bible's influence extended far beyond religion. It became the catalyst for India's socio-economic progress, cultural transformation, and democratic development. Its values inspired reforms in education, justice, and equality, significantly contributing to creating a modern, unified India. *The Bible and the Making of Modern India* is essential for those seeking to understand the intellectual and moral underpinnings of Indian society. By honouring this legacy, Mangalwadi provides insights that inspire hope and change.

As we celebrate Dr. Mangalwadi's lifetime of contributions, his book reminds us to approach history with open minds and hearts, engaging with its lessons for a better future. This foreword is not just a tribute to his work but an invitation to reflect on the enduring relevance of the Bible in shaping societies and advancing humanity.

- **Dr. Richard Howell** is the founder and president of the Caleb Institute, former General Secretary of the Evangelical Fellowship of India and Asia, former vice president of the World Evangelical Alliance, and a founding member of the Global Christian Forum.

Preface

Savarkar was right: "India" is not an Indian idea. No geo-political nation state called India or Bharat had ever existed anywhere in the world until the British colonised the Mughal Empire in 1858. They renamed the Mughal Hindustan "India."

Vinayak Damodar Savarkar was the pioneer of Hindutva ideology. He served as the President of Hindu Mahasabha, which morphed into Jan Sangh and now rules India as the BJP (Bharatiya Janata Party). He believed that Manusmriti—the Law codified by Manu—was and ought to be the law of Hindu society.

The Mughals borrowed the name *"Hindustan"* from Persian *"Hind,"* referring to the region around river Sindh, now in Pakistan. The Greeks changed *"Hind"* to *Indike*. The Latin Bible translated *"Ind"* or *"Indike"* as *"India"* in Esther 1:1 and 8:9.

The idea that "India" was the easternmost province of the Persian empire fascinated fifteenth-century European explorers such as Columbus and Vasco da Gama. For them, to reach India was to see the end of the world. As children of Medieval Europe, the explorers knew the Jewish concept of geography and maps. However, their imperial outlook prevented them from grasping the peculiar Jewish notion of "nation" as a self-governing, sovereign, geo-political state.

Ancient Greece and Rome were city-states which became empires. That means that Europeans knew tribes, *ethne* (people groups), city-states, kingdoms, and empires. They had no experience of the Jewish idea of "nation" and "great nation" (Genesis 12:2).

The Bible began challenging Europe's Holy Roman Empire during the Thirty Years' War (1618-1648). The *Peace of Westphalia* birthed Europe's first two sovereign nations : the Netherlands and Switzerland. North America's thirteen British colonies followed their example. They revolted against the British Empire (1775-1786) and, inspired by the Geneva Bible, became a sovereign nation—not thirteen kingdoms, nor an American Empire.

Nineteenth-century British missionaries introduced the Bible's idea of a nation-state into the Mughal, Maratha, Sikh, Hindu, British, French, and Portuguese kingdoms and empires, thereby forming a nation that we now know as India.

Most educated people do not know of the Bible's role in creating modern India because universities do not teach that the Western Enlightenment was a plagiarised version of the Bible's worldview. Four religions, not three, i.e., Judaism, Christianity, Islam, and secular humanism, have roots in the Bible. Enlightenment humanists thought that human beings were nothing but animals, yet affirmed human dignity and rights as though each human soul was, in fact, made in God's image, different from animals.

The Enlightenment appropriated for itself three key biblical ideas: firstly, the kingship of every believer, or individual sovereignty. Second, it borrowed the Bible's concept of a nation, or national sovereignty. Thirdly, it took the idea of nationalism, that is, love for one's nation.

The Enlightenment embraced the Bible's ideas of citizenship, justice, and the rule of law but made them non-sacred, i.e., secular. The modern emphasis on the development of vernaculars, literature, universal education, the press, the rule of law, human equality and rights, progress, servant-leadership, and ethical businesses all came into India through the Bible.

For example, it was never "self-evident" to any Indian sage or philosopher that all human beings, male and female, were created equal and were endowed by their Creator with inalienable rights. These were divinely revealed truths that came to India with the Bible, as did the law that one Hindu should have only one living spouse or that a wife is not a man's property. Therefore, a husband could not gamble her away—as the Pandavas did in the Mahabharata—nor just abandon her without a legal divorce—as did Mahatma Gandhi and Prime Minister Narendra Modi to their wives.

Most university graduates have no idea that it was the biblical Reformation of the sixteenth century which produced modern democracy, civil and medical services, science, technology, political freedom, and economic development. Hijacking of Christian universities allowed Enlightenment humanists (also called secularists) to brainwash generations into thinking that modern progress came not from the Bible but from human intelligence.

To present the case that modern India is a creation of the Bible, this book builds upon my earlier works, including

(i) *The Father of Modern India: William Carey*, (ii) *Missionary Conspiracy: Letters to a Postmodern Hindu*, and (iii) *India: The Grand Experiment*

It will be followed by a multi-volume, multi-author series called *How the Bible Created Modern India*. Some of my books, such as *The Book That Made Your World: How The Bible Created the Soul of Western Civilisation* and *This Book Changed Everything: The Bible's Amazing Impact on Our World*, discuss the Bible's impact on the modern West. How and why I came to believe the Bible is explained in a forthcoming volume, *My Journey from Philosophy to Revelation*.

Introduction

In his essay on Robert Clive, British historian Lord Thomas Babington Macaulay wrote that British colonialism began in India as "a rule of an evil genie." Once the Mughal Emperor authorised the British East India Company to administer Bengal and collect taxes, it became "a gang of public robbers." What then reformed it?

A generation before Macaulay, during 1785–88, Christian statesman Edmund Burke (1729–1797) had launched the first major moral attack on the Company's corruption. Echoing the biblical-Protestant doctrine of human depravity, Burke complained that India's Governor General, Warren Hastings, was the "Captain General of Iniquity," who never dined without "creating a famine." Hastings' heart was "gangrened to the core," resembling a "Spider of Hell" and a "Ravenous Vulture devouring the carcasses of the dead."

Following Edmund Burke in 1793, William Wilberforce (1759–1833) and his friend Charles Grant (1746–1823) began building the movement to reform the East India Company and Indian society. They were Evangelicals who wanted God's will to be done on earth. God's will, they believed, was revealed by the light of the Bible. Grant had personally seen the horrors of Bengal's famine alluded to by Burke.

The Evangelical campaign in Britain to reform the Company was matched by Bible translators and publishers on the ground in India. These included legendary names such as William Carey, Joshua Marshman, and William Ward in Serampore, Henry Martyn in Kanpur, Claudius Buchanan, and dozens of others in Calcutta. These men laid the foundations upon which the Scottish missionary-statesman, Alexander Duff, built the movement to bring higher education to India. This movement fostered modern India's visionary leaders.

This small book can look only at a few aspects of the history and the culture-changing efforts of Bible-inspired visionaries who demolished traditional fatalism and triggered the nineteenth-century movement known as "India's Renaissance." They transformed dialects into written languages, usually with the Bible as the first published text. The Bible promoted the pursuit of truth, in place of the myths that had enslaved India. Truth by nature liberates.

With the Bible came modern education, extending its benefits to girls and those considered "untouchables." Printing and independent journalism were natural outgrowths of literacy and education. Child-marriage and widow-burning (sati) were outlawed. Widows were freed and encouraged to remarry.

The rule of law and the creation of the Indian Penal Code followed. Property rights, land reforms, modern administration, and a professional army helped make India a nation. Constitutionalism and democracy began to replace the right to rule by force or by birth. The Bible's ideas of human dignity, rights, and equality challenged the caste system. The Bible inspired the movements for socio-economic-political freedom for all. Modern scientific medicine and compassionate nursing took root, bringing healing and hope—even to those suffering from the long-feared affliction of leprosy. Infanticide was criminalised. The worship of nature and demons began to be replaced with scientific inquiry.

Missionary efforts triggered indigenous movements to reform India. These started with well-known figures such as Raja Ram Mohan Roy, Keshab Chandra Sen, Jotiba Phule, Pandita Ramabai, and public intellectuals. Political leaders such as Gandhi, Nehru, and Ambedkar appeared a century after the reformers. They followed the missionaries in thinking of India in biblical terms as a sovereign nation. Many of them absorbed and taught the Bible's work and sexual ethic, including monogamy. Ultimately, during World War II, the tides of history turned when American President Franklin D. Roosevelt enforced the Atlantic Charter, compelling a reluctant Winston Churchill to end British rule in India and all other colonies; setting them free to govern (or misgovern) themselves.

A complementary movement that opposed biblical missions began with Swami Dayanand Saraswati (1824–1883) and Swami Vivekananda (1863–1902). These Indian leaders followed Western Enlightenment in attacking and ridiculing the Bible. Some of them attempted to insert their Bible-derived ideas and values into Hindu and Buddhist scriptures. Others, such as Periyar E. V. Ramasamy (1879–

1973), thought that only atheism could deliver India from oppressive myths. Their rejection of the Bible drove some Indians towards Humanist ideologies of socialism and communism and others towards a revival of Hinduism.

Pandit Jawaharlal Nehru, our first prime minister, embraced socialism and condemned India to corruption and also to decades of the slow so-called "Hindu rate of growth." His naive humanist faith in the innate "goodness of man" corrupted our democratic politics, administration, police, judiciary, press, education, and military.

States with higher levels of literacy and education, such as Bengal and Kerala, went beyond Nehru to elect Communist governments. They drove away industry and businesses, condemning their states to poverty.

Thankfully, in the early 1990s, the stifling and corrupting socialist ideas began to be replaced by more biblical beliefs about economic freedom. That liberated the Indian economy, creating a significant middle class. Poverty, as defined by the World Bank, seemed on track to be cut in half between 1990 and 2014.

But then came the rise of Hindutva, which decided to replace India's semi-Christian, corrupt "secular" governance with an amoral worldview of traditional myths. The consequences have been devastating: a creeping cynicism now grips the nation. Many thoughtful Indians are despairing for the future. Fearing a landscape where power eclipses principle, they urge their children to "quit India" rather than be swallowed by a system where corruption has tainted every institution. Hindutva's pursuit of power has created a toxic alliance of politicians, businessmen, bureaucrats, media elites, and the judiciary. This has deepened the disillusionment. A growing majority is questioning whether India can still produce men and women of integrity, wisdom, and noble character.

Sadly, cut off from the Bible, even Western education has now become incapable of cultivating character. Yet, thankfully, below the surface, the Bible's influence has begun to bear fruit in India. As recently as 2001, Christians were estimated to be only 2.3 percent of the population, that is, about 24 million people. Today, some militant Hindus estimate that the number of Christians may be as high as 84 million, or nearly 8 percent of the population. This figure, albeit difficult to confirm, is being used to persecute recent converts and their pastors. Confirming such numbers is difficult because many followers of Christ, including some who serve as pastors and elders, describe themselves as "Hindu followers of Christ." Some do so out of conviction, to distinguish themselves from westernised "Christians" who do not actually follow Christ.

Other Christian converts label themselves 'Hindus' on paper for less honourable motives, such as educational and economic advantages or to avoid persecution. Nevertheless, across the subcontinent of India, a post-colonial Church has emerged and is being refined in the fires of persecution and discrimination.

Thankfully, the Bible's influence is not confined to church members. Without the Bible, the Christian Church becomes as corrupt as any other institution. Yet the Bible has repeatedly demonstrated its power to transform nations in ancient Israel, in the West, as well as in India. If Indian Christians become serious about prayerfully studying, understanding, obeying, and teaching the Bible, India could become one of the world's greatest nations.

Vishal Mangalwadi
December 20, 2024

Chapter 1

The Bible and the Idea of India

Militant Hindus want to change the name India as well as its Constitution.

In September 2023, India's Federal Government tried to introduce a bill to drop the name "India" through a constitutional amendment.[1] It could not present the bill in the Special Session of Parliament held from September 18 to 22, because it did not have the votes needed to amend the Constitution. More importantly, militant Hinduism has not been able to articulate any convincing arguments that changing the name is necessary.

Militant Hinduism dislikes *India* because it is an alien, non-Indian name. And that is true.

It was not just the name India, but too many of our key ideas also have come to us from the Bible. These anti-Hindu ideas include concepts such as national territory, a political nation-state, the values of nationalism, universal education, the rule of law, equal dignity and human rights.

A Fragmented South Asia

What is India's original, indigenous name?

India never had a name for itself because our ancestors did not develop a concept of a geographic, political nation-state. Therefore, they could not develop the value of loving one's nation, or "nationalism."

Britain colonised much of South Asia during the eighteenth and nineteenth centuries. Prior to that, our people lived as communities of tribes, or varnas. The Portuguese called the varnas "castes." Each tribe or caste had its own deity and religious traditions. No religious law, book, temple, or institution—such as the Church—united these diverse groups.

While some kings erected grand temples, these architectural marvels remained inaccessible to the vast majority of their subjects. Ordinary people were barred from entering these temples. They worshipped in the open or in modest shrines, venerating stones, animals, trees, rivers, mountains, celestial bodies, idols, gurus, kings, and demons. These magnificent temples, rather than serving as places of communal devotion, became instruments of division, reinforcing the rigid hierarchy of caste—separating the privileged from the so-called untouchables.

One reason for excluding the masses was that many temples were centers of Tantric sexual rites, where the elite pursued occult powers, often through esoteric sexual rituals and sacrifices. The justification for this exclusion was cloaked in the rhetoric of ritual purity, branding the "lower" castes as impure and polluting. Crucially, purity was not defined by moral character or deeds but by birth alone. To be born into a lower caste—or even as a woman—was seen as proof of bad karma from past lives, an inescapable fate that determined one's access to the sacred and the social order alike.

Religion reinforced divisions caused by sin, race, tribalism, caste, dialects, and deities. Yet, the common man who worshiped different gods, goddesses, and demons was asked to patronise the same priests, astrologers, mediums, fortune tellers, and tantrics who sought and were believed to possess occult powers of black magic and demons.

In parts of India, castes also came together to watch a religious play or to listen to religious tales and discourses from the same preachers. This, however, was very different from the divine commandments to Israel, which united twelve tribes as one religious community of the mind. The Levites taught all the tribes the same scripture, history, and law in the same language. All Jewish tribes, priests, people, and aristocracy were required to worship in the same temple. That contributed to equality and national unity.

Politics could have united our divided people. That did not happen because, during most of our history, each group lived under its own tribal chief, caste elders, or kings. Brahmin priests encouraged kings to seize their neighbours' territory through the horse sacrifice, known as the *Ashvamedha Yajna*. Even the model ruler, Lord Rama, performed this ritual to increase his territory. His own twin sons, Luv and Kush, resisted their father's territory-expanding ritual, for they did not know that the ruler trying to extend his kingdom was their father, Rama. Their mother Sita had been exiled while they were still in the womb. Such religio-military efforts triggered endless wars, making it impossible for the people to develop the idea of one religion or nation.

The Horse Sacrifice sought to empower a king vis-à-vis other kings in his neighbourhood. That created many conflicts, which weakened Hindu rulers. This allowed Muhammad Ghori, a Muslim, to conquer Delhi in 1192, making it the capital of Muslim India.

At that time, a valiant king, Prithviraj Chauhan, ruled Delhi. Prithviraj's first cousin, Jaichand, was the king of Kannauj. He organised the ritual of horse sacrifice to bring other kings under his rule and taxation. Prithviraj, Delhi's ruler, refused to accept his cousin's sovereignty. That refusal turned the two brothers into rivals. Jealousy motivated Jaichand to invite Muhammad Ghori to come to Delhi and attack his brother Prithviraj.

For brief periods, invaders or emperors united the "religiously" divided people militarily. National unity and progress, however, were not their motives. Usually, their aim was to gather tributes from more people. With the possible exception of Ashoka (304–232 BC), no single empire prior to the British attempted to unite our fragmented communities through a common law, judicial system, universal education, infrastructure of administration, roads, bridges, or tunnels. A people divided by geography, dialects, worship of different deities, and poorly governed by force without their informed consent could not come up with the idea of 'one nation.' Nor could they cultivate the virtue of loving one's nation that did nothing for them.

A terrible implication of India's fragmentation continues in our day. Militant Hindutva tries to unite Hindus around myths and the hatred of Muslims and Christians because it cannot find anything positive in our history around which to bring high- and low-caste Hindus together.

The Name "India" Came From the Bible

In 1492, Christopher Columbus set sail from Spain in search of a sea route to "India." Explorers like him read the name "India" in the Latin Bible, in the book of Esther (1:1 and 8:9). The story of Esther dates back to 479 BC and tells of a young, Jewish woman who had become the queen of Persia (modern Iran). At that time, the Persian Empire extended as far east as the land around the river Sindhu, now in Pakistan.

Europeans learnt about the Persian empire after Alexander the Great travelled to "India" in 326 BC. Historical records of Alexander's conquests fascinated European explorers who imagined that going to India was like going to the end of the world. Although Christopher Columbus never reached India and instead stumbled upon the Americas, the misnomer "Indians" for the native inhabitants persisted.

It was through European explorers that the concept of a geographic India came to be. In 1498, six years after Columbus discovered the Americas, another European explorer, Vasco da Gama set sail in search of a sea route to India. He landed in Calicut, in present-day Kerala, in south-western India.

It is important to note that when Vasco da Gama arrived, he encountered people who had never heard of a nation called "India" and did not identify as "Indians." Even in the 1600s, the term "India" was not widely associated with South Asia.

British merchants established the British East India Company in 1600, followed two years later by Dutch merchants forming the Dutch East India Company, aided by theologian Petrus Plancius. However, neither company initially aimed to trade with what we now call "India"— their primary interest was in "Indonesia," then considered the true "Indian Asia."

Since the Dutch secured dominance in Indonesia first, the British turned their focus to South Asia, eventually laying the groundwork for modern India. Ironically, even Europeans of that era did not conceive of South Asia as "India"— the concept arrived with them and evolved over time.

Hindutva dislikes the name *India* because it is an alien name and idea. The vision of India as a political nation-state developed three centuries after Vasco da Gama. Protestant missionaries, civil servants, and their proteges were the first to conceptualise India as a nation-state.

The Latin name *India*, as already mentioned, came out of Sindhu, the river that originates in the Himalayas and flows mostly through present-day Pakistan. In modern atlases, this river is called the *Indus*. The Persians who ruled the land around Sindhu found it difficult to pronounce "S." Therefore, they called the river "Hindu."

For Persians, the regions around the river Sindhu became Hindustan. They termed various religions and cultures of Hindustan "Hindu." That is why Hindu scholars prefer not to identify their religion as "Hindu." These days they like using the Buddhist label "Sanatan" for what is still called "Hinduism." Be that as it may, the relevant point is that the Hebrew Bible changed Persian *Hindu* to *Hodu*. Later, the Greeks pronounced the Persian *Hindu* as *Indu* or *Indike*. Western Europe read the Latin Bible, which changed Greek *Indu*, *Indic*, or *Indike* into *India*.

Hindustan

In 1858, the British Crown began governing what Muslims used to call *Hindustan*. Some British Bible translators and the men who ruled Bengal were already using the biblical name *India* for what the Mughals called *Hindustan*. William Carey's journal that merged into the Calcutta *Statesman* was called *Friend of India*. The name was meant to make a distinction between the East India Company and the missionary movement. The Company was in India to trade and rule. Missionaries had come to the subcontinent to serve God and their neighbours.

In 1947, the colony that the British had called India became an independent nation-state. I was born two years later and grew up in the northern states of Uttar Pradesh and Madhya Pradhesh. All school-aged children were taught early on to sing the words of north India's most popular nationalist song:

Sare Jahan se achha Hindustan hamara Hum bulbulen hain iski, yeh gulsitan hamara.

Translated into English, the opening stanza:

Better than the entire world is our Hindustan,
We are its nightingales, and it is our garden abode.

Sir Muhammad Iqbal (1877–1938) composed that song in Urdu in 1904, over a decade before Mahatma Gandhi returned from South Africa to lead the national struggle for independence.

Iqbal's song served as an anthem of the Gandhi-led independence struggle. It shaped the principle for which militant Hindus killed Mahatma Gandhi. Take, for example, Iqbal's sixth stanza,

Religion does not teach us to bear animosity among ourselves We are of Hind, our homeland is Hindustan.

In Iqbal's own words,

Mazhab nahīn

sikhātā āpas men

bair rakhnā

Hindī hain

ham, watan hai Hindustān

hamārā

Iqbal's song made "Hindustan" the most beloved name for our nation. It inspired popular slogans such as *Jai Hind* (Victory to Hind). However, the Constitution did not name the new nation *Hindustan*.

Why not?

The sad answer is that the Constitution was drafted after the Hindu-Muslim-Sikh riots killed a million or more people and threw over 10 million Hindustanis out of their homes.

Iqbal first composed his song as a tribute to Hindustani children, embracing them all, regardless of religion. But by 1910, his youthful idealism had begun to crack. Reality forced him to reconsider. In 1930, he traveled to my home city of Allahabad—where I grew up decades later in the 1950s and 60s. In Allahabad Iqbal delivered a speech to the Muslim League that would change history. No longer just a poet, Iqbal had become the voice of realism. He put forth the idea of a separate Muslim nation, believing that Islam and Hinduism lacked a shared vision. He could no longer imagine a unified garden where flowers of vastly different kinds could flourish together.

His new vision, shared by some Hindus, laid the groundwork for the two-nation theory, which ultimately led to the violent partition of South Asia in 1947. Mahatma Gandhi knew the hatred that ruled our hearts. However, he refused to accept that hatred could define Hindustan's destiny. He fought instead for love and justice, believing they alone could hold the nation together.

But the spirit of hatred proved stronger. It did not just tear apart a land that had lived under British law—it also silenced Gandhi himself. In 1948, he fell to the bullets of a Hindu extremist, just as a million others perished in the bloodshed of Partition. With that, Iqbal's once-innocent dream of a united Hindustan—a garden where all could bloom—was buried forever.

The Constituent Assembly that voted to rename Hindustan as "India, that is, Bharat," was elected in 1946, a year before Independence. The Constitution it wrote came into effect on January 26, 1950. The Assembly considered suggestions to name India "Bharatvarsha", "Aryavrata," or "Jambudvipa." After due deliberations, it settled on two names: "*India*, that is, *Bharat*, shall be a Union of States." The alternative, "*Bharat* that is *India*," did not find enough support. For no nation called *Bharat* had ever existed in the subcontinent. In contrast, "India" had been a British colony since 1858.

Later in this book we shall see that the Bible-based English literature promoted the Jewish idea of "nation" and the biblical value called "nationalism." It created the political environment that birthed "nationalist" organisations such as:

- The Indian National Association founded in Calcutta on 25 September 1875

- The Indian League in 1875 under the chairmanship of Rev Krishna Mohan Banerjee, which merged into the Indian Association, and the
- The Indian National Congress founded in December 1885 by a retired British Civil Servant, Allan Octavian Hume.

Much before the Constituent Assembly debated India's name, Pandit Jawaharlal Nehru, who became our first prime minister, had already wrestled with the identity of the nation about to be born. During World War II, from 1942 to 1946, Nehruji had been imprisoned in Ahmednagar Fort. There he wrote his classic treatise, *The Discovery of India*. Panditji searched for but did not find an indigenous name for Hindustan. Therefore, he stuck with the Bible-derived name *India*. Other nationalists shared his perspective.

Geography

None of the Hindu Scriptures identify South Asia with a geographic name because the philosophies, now clustered together as Hinduism or Sanatan, had no interest in geography. "Jambudvipa" came the closest. But "dvipa" means island, and South Asia is not an island. Therefore, eminent historians such as John Keay and William Dalrymple think that "Jambudvipa" may refer to the island of Java. Buddhism had reached Java as early as the first century after Christ. The best-developed Hindu philosophies took no interest in geography because they considered creation to be Maya—an illusion. Their goal was to be delivered from Maya.

By contrast, the Bible from its opening chapter affirms God's creation to be real and good. It describes the geography of the Garden of Eden, with four rivers named Pishon, Gihon, Tigris, and Euphrates (Genesis 2:11–14), where Adam and Eve were placed to be its stewards. They were given the task of naming the animals and tending the garden. In Genesis 10, the Bible describes the formation of nations in distinct territories. Later in Genesis 13 and 15, God delineates the specific territory He promised to give Abraham as his nation. The sixth book of the Bible, Joshua, goes into the boundaries of the territory each Israeli tribe was to be given. Because of this geography-conscious background, the apostle Paul introduced the Jewish idea of a geographic nation to the

Greeks in Acts 17:26–27. Until then, Greeks had only known city-states, empires, or people groups. The Bible's idea of a nation with stated borders began changing Europe only after the Peace of Westphalia in 1648.

The Bible portrays empires as diabolical because they covet their neighbours' real estate and go to war. It presents nations with defined borders as God's prescription for international peace. Since God emphasises geographic boundaries for nations, the British East India Company, in 1767, established the first ever scientific institution in India, called The Survey of India. One of its principal tasks was map-making.

In 1911, the Bible's worldview, which took God-given geographic borders seriously, gave India the first song that defined the national borders of pre-Partition India. This Bengali song, entitled "Jana Gana Mana," by Nobel laureate Rabindranath Tagore, was translated into English on February 28, 1919. It is impossible to miss the poem's theistic (biblical) ethos:

Thou art the ruler of the minds of all people,
dispenser of India's destiny.
Thy name rouses the hearts of the Punjab, Sindh, Gujarat and Maratha,
of the Dravida, Orissa and Bengal.
It echoes in the hills of the Vindhyas and Himalayas,
mingles in the music of the Yamuna and Ganges
and is chanted by the waves of the Indian Sea.
They pray for thy blessings and sing thy praise.
The saving of all people waits in thy hand,
thou dispenser of India's destiny.
Victory, Victory, Victory to thee!

Tagore's song, which remains our national anthem, excluded Kashmir from India's geography. Why? It did so because the Bengali poet—the first non-European to win a Nobel prize in any category and the first lyricist to win a Nobel Prize in Literature—borrowed his providential geography from the British Parliament's Stamp Act of 1899. The

British won Kashmir from its Sikh ruler and sold it to Jammu's Hindu governor. Therefore, the Stamp Act excluded Kashmir from the geography of India as it was defined at that time. The important point here is that Tagore did not find India's geography outlined in any Hindu scriptures. These named their holy sites spread all over South Asia but did not name India or define its territory. The *Sanatan Dharma* (Hinduism) knew lots of kingdoms but lacked any concept of a nation, Hindu or otherwise.

The Bible and the Birth of Indian Nationalism

The absence of the very idea of India made it impossible for a religious, political, or literary movement to cultivate love for the nation of India. The sad reality is that religion and politics were the chief means of dividing India. Sanskrit could have united India since most Brahmin priests memorised it. However, the Brahmins kept it as their monopoly—a means of exclusion and discrimination.

The first Indian to write nationalist poetry was Henry Louis Vivian Derozio (1809-1831). He was an Anglo-Indian who taught in Calcutta's Hindu College and died at the age of 22.

Michael Madhusudan Dutt (1824-1873), a Hindu convert to Christ, is considered the "Father of Nationalist Poetry" because, even though he was fluent in many languages, he wrote his nationalist poems in Bengali. That began the literary tradition that gave us "Vande Mataram" (1880), the nationalist poem of Bakim Chandra Chatterjee, which was included in his 1882 novel *Anand Math*. Chatterjee, incidentally, was a British civil servant.

Following "Vande Mataram" came "Sare Jahan Se Achha" by Sir Mohammad Iqbal (1904) and "Jana Gana Mana" by Rabindranath Tagore (1911). None of these nationalist poems were inspired by Hindu or Muslim scriptures. Nationalist poetry was the Indian response to English education, specifically to British nationalist poets such as William Wordsworth (1770-1850) and Alfred, Lord Tennyson (1809-1892). World War II made *"nationalism"* a dirty word in Europe because the Fascists deceptively rebranded what was actually German imperialism as so-called *"nationalism."*

However, pre-Fascist English poets derived the virtue of nationalism from the Bible. Consider, for example, Psalm 137:

> By the waters of Babylon, there we sat down and wept,
> when we remembered Zion.
>
> On the willows there we hung up our lyres. For there our captors required of us songs,
> and our tormentors, mirth, saying,
> "Sing us one of the songs of Zion!"
>
> How shall we sing the Lord's song in a foreign land? If I forget you, O Jerusalem,
> let my right hand forget its skill! Let my tongue stick to the roof of my mouth,
> if I do not remember you,
> if I do not set Jerusalem above my highest joy!

Or, take Psalm 102:

> But you, O Lord, are enthroned forever;
> You are remembered throughout all generations.
> You will arise and have pity on Zion;
> it is the time to favour her;
> the appointed time has come.
> For your servants hold her stones dear
> and have pity on her dust.
> Nations will fear the name of the Lord,
> and all the kings of the earth will fear your glory.
> For the Lord builds up Zion;
> He appears in his glory

The Bible's nationalism is very different from fascist nationalism. In the Bible, God is the creator of the nations. Therefore, true Biblical nationalism is God-centered. As such, it is joyous, grateful and repentant.

Germany's fascist nationalism was born at the end of the nineteenth century, and captured the public imagination in the twentieth century because German theologians had effectively undermined the Bible. Fascism corrupted biblical nationalism by making it man, race, and land-centered loyalty.

Contrast this to the Old Testament prophets Isaiah, Jeremiah, Ezekiel, Daniel, and Amos, who were nationalists but condemned Israel's immorality. They loved their nation and wanted their people to be godly. European fascism masquerading as nationalism, on the other hand, was arrogant imperialism. It was not love for one's own nation but greed, which sought to take over neighbours' lands and incited two world wars. The Third Reich's ideology made no attempt to make their nation live by God's law. Neither does Hindu nationalism make any effort today to reform India's corrupt governance.

Jewish nationalism was best exhibited by Daniel, Nehemiah, and Esther. Each of them excelled in serving non-Jewish emperors who had conquered their country and taken their people into captivity. These Old Testament heroes risked their lives to love and serve their own people without hating others. True nationalists love their neighbours as themselves because God called his children to be a blessing to all the nations of the earth, including their enemies. God began to fulfill the promise He repeated to each patriarchs—Abraham, Isaac, and Jacob—through Abraham's descendants. They initiated India's Renaissance.

Chapter 2

The Bible
and India's Renaissance[1]

Ancient India had many cultures, most of them oral. While Buddhist scholars wrote down their scriptures, the oldest and most sacred of Hindu scriptures, the Vedas, were unwritten. Buddhist scholars used various scripts and languages, but Sanskrit, the sacred and sophisticated language of the Hindu priests, had no script. Kharosthi and Brahmi scripts used by Buddhists died between the third and seventh centuries after Christ. Therefore, when the British arrived, India did not have a single scholar who could read the edicts on the Ashoka Pillars, which had been carved prior to 230 BC. Those scripts were deciphered by English Indologist James Prinsep in 1837–38.

Sanskrit could have united India, but it could not become India's national language. As a matter of fact, it couldn't even become the mother tongue of the priestly caste of Brahmins. This was because priests refused to teach it to women, even their wives. Women, in turn, could not teach it to their children

Oral cultures can develop fantastic stories. Sacred myths evolve from generation to generation, but unwritten tradition cannot document history. Myths have to be believed. They cannot be debated or scruti-

---

1. I am grateful to Prof. Ashish Alexander for his contribution to this chapter.

nised. This is also why ancient India has such scant documentation about Christianity's early influence.

One tradition maintains that after Babylonian emperor Nebuchadnezzar died in 562 BC, some Jews arrived in Cochin, South India. The Hindu king gave them permission—in perpetuity—to live, build synagogues, and own property. In the more poetic expression of those days, they were permitted to live "as long as the world and moon exist." These Jews settled down in what is now Kerala.

Another group, Bene Israel from Judea, claims that their ancestors arrived 2,100 years ago because a shipwreck stranded seven families south of modern-day Mumbai. More exiles came after AD 70, when the Romans destroyed the Jewish temple in Jerusalem.

According to credible traditions, Christ's apostle, St. Thomas came to India in the middle of the first century. The earliest known text that describes Thomas's time in India is *The Acts of Thomas*. It describes Thomas's travels around India, bringing Christianity. According to this text, Thomas founded seven churches.

A number of third- and fourth-century Roman writers mention Thomas's trip to India. These include Ambrose of Milan, Gregory of Nazianzus, Jerome, and Ephrem the Syrian. Eusebius of Caesarea records that his teacher Pantaneus visited a Christian community in India in the second century.

An organised Christian presence in India dates to the arrival of East Syrian settlers and missionaries from Persia around the third century AD. They were members of the *Church of the East*, i.e., the Nestorian Church. Saint Thomas Christians, numbering approximately 12 million today in India, trace the growth of their community to the arrival of the Nestorian Thomas of Cana from the Middle East. This migration is said to have occurred sometime between the fourth and eighth centuries.

From the early fourth century, the Patriarch of the Church of the East provided India with clergy, holy texts, and ecclesiastical infrastructure. Theophilus (known as "Theophilus the Indian") travelled to India in AD 354. His travels were recorded by Greek historian Philostorgius.

He told the Saviour's good news in various parts of India. The rise of Islam made such missions difficult because, periodically, Islamic rulers cut India off from connection with Persian and Mesopotamian Christianity.

Contact With European Christianity

Muslim blockades of the land trade routes forced Europeans to develop sea routes to India. In 1492, Christopher Columbus tried to find the sea route to India but landed in the Americas. In 1498, Vasco da Gama won that glory for Portuguese explorers. He met with Saint Thomas Christians in India. At that time, they were in a tenuous position, trying to survive in the spice trade, protected by their private militia. India was divided into far too many little kingdoms to facilitate fear-free trading in goods and ideas.

British merchants became involved in India through the East India Company (also known as "the Company"). It was chartered in 1600 by Queen Elizabeth I. The Company was created twelve years after the defeat of the Spanish Armada, which made England Europe's premier sea power. Wealthy merchants and aristocrats, not the government, owned the Company. That means that the government's control was only an indirect, political oversight of a legitimate business.

In 1707, the East India Company became a British joint-stock company formed to pursue trade with the "East Indies." Mostly it traded with China and other parts of Southeast Asia. The Company grew to account for half of the world's trade, particularly in basic commodities that included cotton, silk, indigo dye, salt, tea, spices, and opium.

Following the Battle of Plassey in Bengal (1757) and the Battle of Buxar in Bihar (1764), the Mughal Emperor gave the Company administrative authority over Bengal, which then included Bihar, Bangladesh, Orissa, and Assam. The Company's private army began to exercise military power. Its merchants gained control of some of the richest areas of India. After the great Indian Revolt of 1857, the responsibility to govern India was taken over directly by the British Crown.

Missionaries

Britain's spiritual renewal during the revival led by John Wesley (1703–1791) generated the religious energy to reform Britain. Under pressure from the East India Company, the British Parliament banned missionaries from going to Bengal. Everyone knew that the Company's interest in extracting wealth will conflict with the missionary interest in serving Indians. Yet, it became impossible to restrain heroic souls who felt called by God to take Gospel Light to the world.

Roman Catholic missionaries, especially the Jesuits, preceded British Protestants by more than two centuries. Their Order was founded in 1534 for "whoever desires to serve as a soldier of God." The Pope had conferred upon the Portuguese government certain authority in ecclesiastical matters in foreign territories that they conquered. Invoking that authority, the Jesuits entered into treaties and decrees in an attempt to dominate Saint Thomas Christians. At first, the Portuguese subjection of the Saint Thomas Christians was measured. After 1552, it became aggressive, giving greater authority to the Church than to God's Word.

The sixteenth-century Protestant Reformation took the Bible out of monasteries and made it the handbook of every person who wanted to know and serve God. The Bible began the intellectual renewal of the masses that made Protestant nations stronger than their Orthodox and Roman Catholic rivals. The Bible, for example, taught Englishmen, "He also that is slack in his work is brother to him that is a destroyer [waster]" (Proverbs 18:9). As sociologists such as Max Weber have noted, it was the Bible that taught the common man to be diligent in his work. The Lord Jesus himself taught that a good, wise, and faithful servant, approved and commended by God, was a diligent worker. He will be given authority to govern. (e.g., Matthew 24:45 and 25:21). Likewise, the Apostle Paul commanded believers to "redeem the time" (Ephesians 5:16; Colossians 4:5). To redeem something or someone is to put considerable value on it; to buy it—not waste it. Paul also commanded, "...*If any man would not work, neither should he eat*" (2 Thessalonians 3:10).

The Bible's work ethic made England a powerful nation because the people who wanted to obey God began to use time thoughtfully. Simple people kept private journals and noted down how they had utilised every hour of every day. When they wasted time, they repented privately and even publicly. This attitude of time management was very different from Hindu religiosity, which worshiped the god of time as "Kaal." Stories are told of mythical Indian sages who sat in silent meditation for 144 years to acquire occult powers. However, the Protestant work ethic enabled Christian nations to become more powerful than cultures that waste, rather than responsibly manage, time. India's interaction with the Bible began its intellectual, moral, and cultural renaissance.

A Linguistic Revolution to Empower People

Culture is the externalisation of thoughts and ideas. We think in language. Thinking goes beyond memorisation of sacred mantras. India's intellectual renaissance began with the linguistic revolution, pioneered by a Baptist missionary, William Carey (1761-1834). This British cobbler-turned-linguist came to Bengal in 1793.

Eight decades prior to William Carey, a German missionary, Bartholomaus Ziegenbalg (1683–1719), had already come to Tranquebar, now called Tharangambadi in the Mayiladuthurai district of Tamil Nadu. Along with his colleague Heinrich Plütschau, Ziegenbalg translated the New Testament and part of the Old Testament into Tamil. Their mission, patronised by Denmark's Lutheran king, brought a printing press and made paper in order to print the Bible. This pioneering effort, however, did not begin India's linguistic revolution. In 1845, the Danes sold Tranquebar to the British East India Company.

When Carey arrived in Bengal, the Mughal Empire had three classical languages: Persian, Arabic, and Sanskrit. Muslim and Hindu elites had turned these languages into walls of discrimination, depriving the common man of the power of knowledge. Empowerment of the common man began when missionaries turned Indian dialects into written languages that could communicate great ideas. This Protestant linguistic movement shattered centuries of privilege, democratising learning and empowering the masses like never before.

Brahmin priests memorised Sanskrit scriptures, not for intellectual thought but for performing religious rituals. Likewise, Muslim masses spoke local dialects while their religious leaders memorised the Quran in Arabic. Muslims ruled much of India for seven centuries, yet they did not make Arabic the people's language of learning for imparting facts and ideas.

Two centuries before Carey came to Bengal, Mughal Emperors had made Persian their court language. Their mother tongue was Chagatai, not Persian. Though they ruled Bengal, they took no interest in developing Bengali. Nor did they popularise Arabic and Sanskrit. Persian was a great language, but the Mughals made it their court language, partly to make it difficult for Arabic- and Pashto-speaking Muslims to learn state secrets.

The Mughals gave the administrative authority, or Diwani, over Bengal to the East India Company in 1765. Yet until 1800, British merchants and rulers took little interest in the Bengali dialects spoken by the people they governed. The only educational institution that the British Company established was the Calcutta Madrasa (1780–81) under Warren Hastings. It was created to teach Arabic, Persian, and Islamic law. Arts and science, literature, and the humanities found no place in the curricula.

Ten years later, in 1791, the British Company, not Hindu ashrams, established the Banaras Sanskrit College in the state of Varanasi. It was only after two centuries in 1974 that the government of India upgraded it to become Sampurnanand Sanskrit University.

This religious and political indifference to India's intellectual progress changed when British evangelicals responded to Charles Grant's appeal to Christians to assume the moral responsibility to bless the people of India. Grant's *Observations on the Asiatic Subjects of Great Britain* (1792) inspired an evangelical Member of Parliament, William Wilberforce, to campaign for India's education. Grant and Wilberforce argued that it was immoral for Britain to send only merchants and mercenaries to India. Britain must also send educators who would, by definition, be missionaries. In Grant and Wilberforce's time, education was a ministry of the Church. No such thing as non-sacred (i.e., secular) education existed anywhere in the world.

Education was under the authority of the Church because the Bible asserts that God "wants all men to be saved and come to the knowledge of the truth" (1 Timothy 2:4). The idea that every child needed to be educated was a practical application of the New Testament's teaching that every child of God needed to serve his heavenly Father as a priest and manage God's kingdom on earth as a prince or king. European reformers recognised that fulfilling God's will required knowing Him, and knowing Him required studying His word. This conviction drove the translation of Scripture into the mother tongues of the people

This theological outlook had been transforming European dialects into modern literary languages, including German, English, and French.

The campaign for India's education initiated by Charles Grant and led by Wilberforce was understood in the light of the Bible's theology of language and education. The British Parliament understood that sending educators to India meant sending missionaries who were simultaneously linguists and educators. While the Company's "mission" was financial profit, Christian missionaries would go to serve God and the people of the Indian subcontinent. Enriching people's dialects to become literary languages became the foundation stones of India's moral, social, intellectual, and economic awakening.

Wilberforce began the campaign for South Asia's education in 1793. (At that time, no nation called "India" existed in the political sense of the word.) Twenty years later, in 1813, the British Parliament approved a new Charter of the East India Company, requiring the Company to spend Rs. 100,000 per year for the education of the people of Bengal.

How was this money to be used? The Company leaders decided to use the funds to establish a Sanskrit college in Calcutta. This would provide employment to Pandits and win their support for the Company. The Company was already running a Sanskrit college in Banaras. The decision to establish a second Sanskrit college triggered the "Language Controversy."

Many agreed with William Carey's view that reforming India required, first and foremost, developing vernacular languages spoken by the people. The Classicists argued that teaching Sanskrit, Persian, and

Arabic would develop the vernaculars. The Anglicists disagreed. They proposed that instruction in English would better develop the vernaculars because it would enable access to all the literature and science in Britain.

The conflict was resolved by Lord Thomas Babbington Macaulay's *Minute Upon Indian Education* in 1835. Macaulay favoured teaching English in order to enrich the vernacular, including Bengali. Charles Grant had already suggested that line of thinking in 1792. Carey's protegees, Raja Ram Mohan Roy in 1814 and Alexander Duff in 1830, had also begun championing English education. Macaulay's brother-in-law, Charles Trevelyan, joined that cause in 1831.

Raja Ram Mohan Roy's Opposition to Sanskrit

Before William Carey and his team established the Serampore Mission in 1800, Raja Ram Mohan Roy had gone to William Carey to learn English and teach him Sanskrit. Later, he came to Serampore to help translate the Bible into Sanskrit—a collaboration that profoundly influenced his thinking. That interaction so changed Roy that he became a vocal opponent and a fierce critic of the British plan to establish Calcutta Sanskrit College.

On 11 December 1823, Roy wrote to the British Prime Minister, William Pitt, that the decision to teach the "Sanskrit system of education would be best calculated to keep this country in darkness." Perpetuating Sanskrit education, Roy argued, would be contrary to the spirit of the great movement that had required the Company to invest money for the opening up of the Indian mind. Even though Roy was a Brahmin and a Sanskrit scholar, he opposed the Company hiring Pundits to teach Sanskrit. The British policy, he argued, ought to be to "promote a more liberal and enlightened system of instruction, embracing mathematics, natural philosophy, chemistry, and anatomy, with other useful sciences."

Roy knew that the Pundits' monopoly of Sanskrit had stunted and enslaved the Indian mind. While language is the God-given means to open and enhance the mind, the Bible teaches that God Himself is the Word (*Logos*) and, therefore, mind and language are God's greatest gifts to humanity. Language unites God's children into a community of shared ideas and values. It sets us apart from animals that are herded together by instinct, fear, and force. Language allows us to improve our community by thinking critically in order to seek truth and wisdom. This is necessary to steward our Father's creation.

Language should not be, Roy asserted, what Pundits had reduced it to —a means of uncritical memorisation of mantras. Why did they reduce language to this? Because they did not seek truth. They wanted occult powers to appease gods and control demons. As Mahatma Phule put it a few decades later, priests memorise Sanskrit mantras to intimidate people into paying for the appeasement of unknown gods.

Roy knew firsthand that Sanskrit had closed the Indian mind. No Sanskrit scholar had written books on nature, science, medicine, agriculture, technology, law, history, geography, or governance. Nor had any Sanskrit scholar developed any Indian dialect into a literary language. Instead, as Ziegenbalg had noted a century earlier, the Pundits had imposed a hierarchical system of high and low varnas that precluded developing the common man's intellectual potential. The Aryans came to India with Sanskrit and Vedas. They were proud of their scriptures but made absolutely no effort to translate Sanskrit scriptures into the languages of the people.

Swami Dayananda Saraswati, the founder of Arya Samaj—deemed heretical by most Hindus—was the first to publish selected parts of the Vedas into Hindi in 1875. Dayananda was responding to H. H. Wilson's translation of the Vedas into English that began in 1850 and Max Muller's translation published in 1856.

Sir Charles Wilkins (1749-1836) was the first person to translate the Bhagavad Gita into English in 1785. No Hindi edition of Gita was published until the early 20th century. Goswami Tulsidas (1511-1623) was a rare exception. He paraphrased the Sanskrit epic *Ramayana* into the Awadhi dialect, renaming it *Ramcharit Manas*. Awadhi was spoken around Varanasi and Ayodhya. For his audacity to compose their sacred story in a commonplace dialect, other Pundits refused to acknowledge Tulsidas' work as part of the canon of Hindu scripture. In any case, the people who spoke Awadhi could not read it. There were no schools to teach non-Brahmin men to read or write in their mother tongues. Tulsidas' work became influential much later, only when it began to be dramatised as the folk reenactment, *Ramlila*.

It was William Carey, the British cobbler turned missionary, who translated the *Ramayana* into English. In the late nineteenth century Rev. Samuel Kellogg (1839–1899), an American Presbyterian missionary, fused Awadhi with ten other dialects to create Hindi grammar as we know it today. Kellogg lived in my hometown of Allahabad, just 120 kilometers north of Tulsidas' Banaras. Contemporary Allahabadi natives speak Kellogg's Hindi, but in contrast no one in Allahabad without formal instruction in Awadhi can understand a single stanza of Tulsidas' *Ramcharit Manas*.

Bible-Inspired Linguistic Revolutions

Samuel Kellogg, who created the Hindi grammar that we use today, followed Carey's monumental linguistic revolution. He completed the work of his predecessors. John Gilchrist, a Scottish naval surgeon in the East India Company, had combined a number of dialects to create what he called *Hindustani*.

One successor of Gilchrist was Henry Martyn, an Anglican priest and chaplain who had sailed east with the Company. Martyn himself had been inspired by the missionary life of William Carey, and used other pre-existing dialects as well as Persian and Arabic to translate the Bible into the language we now know as Urdu. Kellogg, encouraged by several Sanskrit scholars, followed up on Gilchrist and Martyn's groundbreaking work to create Hindi grammar. He used Tulsidas' *Ramcharit Manas* as the literary base for creating modern Hindi, which has become north India's *de facto* "national" language.

Translating the Bible into languages actually spoken by the people was a monumental grassroots revolution. It did for India what the Protestant Reformation had done for Europe's education, literature, culture, economy, and governance through the undertaking of reformers such as John Wycliffe, Martin Luther, and William Tyndale.

Old Tamil had developed, but Bengali, Urdu, Hindi, and other languages did not exist when William Carey arrived in India. Bharatendu

Harishchandra (1850–1885), the first Indian writer of modern Hindi, was born eleven years after Kellogg. Although he was the first native Indian to write in Hindi, Bharatendu was not a Brahmin from a scholarly caste. He was a Vaishya -Agarwal - from a mercantile caste.

Likewise, Munshi Premchand, India's first Hindi novelist to publish prose in the style of literary realism, was a Srivastava, i.e., a Kayastha (or Shudra). The Kayasthas today are classified as educated, therefore, "forward" castes. The term "forward caste" is a relatively recent political category, however, and is distinct from the ancient religious category of "high" caste. Had he been born in an earlier century, Premchand would not have received an education.

To deprive people of the ability to read, think, and write in their own language is a strategy which condemns them to ignorance. This makes them easy prey to unscrupulous clergy, who are usually in league with the aristocracy. Ignorance violates their innate dignity of being made in the image of an omniscient Creator. The Bible that liberated Europe from its oppressive religions also began India's transformation.

The Bible's enormous impact on every Indian language, literacy, literature, and education has been best studied by Dr. Babu Verghese in his book *Let There Be India: Impact of the Bible on Nation Building*. Dr. Ashish Alexander illustrates this thesis with two examples.

I: Baptists and Bengali

The advocate-in-chief of the Indian vernaculars, William Carey, worked in Serampore and Calcutta. I call him the Father of Modern India. Carey fused several dialects to create Bengali as a literary language. He had translated the Bible into Bengali before opening his mission in Serampore in 1800. Writing in Bengali a century later, Rabindranath Tagore went on to win the first Nobel Prize for India.

Merely a hundred years before Tagore, his own city of Calcutta—which became the capital of Bengal province—did not have a single qualified teacher of Bengali. Bengal did not lack learned Pandits, but they considered Bengali a language fit only for women and demons. Mr. Sushil Kumar De points out in his study, *Bengali Literature in the Nineteenth Century: 1757-1857*, that it was Carey and his missionary colleagues who "raised the language from the debased condition of an unsettled dialect to the character of a regular and permanent form of speech." The Nobel Prize Committee noted that Bengali songs of the *Gitanjali* display both the influence of Carey's language as well as the Bible's theistic worldview.

In Serampore and especially in Calcutta, William Carey started translating the Bible in multiple languages with help from Pandits who taught languages to civil servants at Fort William College. When some Company directors began to object that their profits were being used to translate the Bible, Charles Grant and others organised the British and Foreign Bible Society to finance the translation work. Serampore Mission Press printed these vernacular Bibles and invented the fonts for different scripts.

The Mission also manufactured the paper needed for printing. The fonts, the paper, and the printing press began to open the Indian mind because, as we will see in other chapters, the missionary movement undergirded that historic effort by spreading literacy, printing textbooks for schools, and initiating journalism.

The Indian elite had kept classic languages—Sanskrit, Persian, and Arabic—for themselves. Missionaries allowed them to keep their monopoly but went on to empower the people by enriching vernacular languages. Today only about 25,000 Indians speak Sanskrit, while 234 million people speak Bengali as their native tongue. Hindi is spoken by about 585 million people!

William Carey agreed with Alexander Duff and others that enriching vernaculars required teaching English to the people who wanted to develop their mother tongue. However, his mission also noted that the enthusiasm for learning English among the upper-caste Indians was problematic. They did not learn English for the general welfare of the society. Their objective was selfish—namely personal and professional advancement. They observed that a little knowledge of English was turning the "finest youth" of Bengal into "mercenary copyists." They remained ignorant of their own mother tongue of Bengali, and unconcerned about the wisdom, beauty, goodness, and truth that access to the English language and literature offered. The East India Company needed hirelings and therefore taught English to some youth. But those efforts would never have produced a Roy or a Tagore. They were the fruit of the Bengali Bible.

II: Presbyterians and Punjabi

Stationed in Bengal to the east, William Carey also strove to translate the Bible for the regions he never personally visited. He published Punjabi grammar in 1812, followed by the first Punjabi Bible in 1815. The Serampore Mission Press printed the first ever prose work in the Gurmukhi script, the Punjabi New Testament that year.

American Presbyterians were the first missionaries to set foot in Punjab in 1834. They discovered to their surprise that Carey's translation of the Bible was already circulating in that region of northwest India. Noting room for improvement, they began a fresh translation of the Bible in Punjabi, while also preparing a new grammar and the first dictionary. The new,comprehensive Punjabi grammar was published by John Newton in 1851. The other significant work, a dictionary by Levi Janvier, came out in 1854. Yet another translation of the New Testament was published in 1868, marking the transition from traditional to modern Punjabi.

The Bible translation movement made it possible for the East India Company to replace Persian with local vernaculars as official administrative languages. With the passage of Act No. 29 of 1837, Hindustani was declared the administrative language in Bihar, the Northwest Provinces, and the Central Provinces. Bengali and Odia were declared the languages of business administration and revenue for their respective territories. Punjabi should have been designated as the official language of Punjab. However, languages need patrons. Without institutional support, languages rarely develop and sustain themselves. Due to political considerations and the still-nascent language of Punjabi, the Punjab government of the time made Urdu its official language. Punjabi, the people's language, did not become the language of the educated elite. . The court language of Maharaja Ranjit Singh, the greatest Sikh ruler of the time, was Persian. Sikh writers in other principalities wrote in Braj, the popular literary language of north India. Urdu and Persian continued to hold sway over the educated elite of Punjab. The movement that empowered the mother tongue of the masses was the Bible movement. Christian missionaries changed Punjab because the Bible taught them that God wanted all people to know the liberating power of truth.

Official policies and the prejudices of the native elite did not deter missionary scholars. They continued to publish and print the good news of salvation in Punjabi. American Presbyterians and later the Christian Missionary Society (CMS) became the alternate patrons of the Punjabi language in the nineteenth century. Their labour made it possible for the later resurgent Sikh movement to promote and develop the Punjabi language.

Punjab progressed because the missionaries did not limit their effort to publishing the Bible and devotional texts. They introduced a variety of literary modes to Punjabi: one-act plays, short stories, and especially the novel. The first Punjabi novel, *Jyotiruday,* came out of the missionary quarters in 1882. Sixteen years later the first novel from the pen of native Sikh writer Bhai Vir Singh, *Sundari,* was published. Biased minds with fixed presuppositions find it difficult to give credit where it is due. Yet, the eminent Punjabi scholar Gurcharan Singh Arshi, acknowledged the impact of the Bible and missionaries in these words:

"Though Christian missionaries came with the intention of propagation and advancement of [their] religion, in that endeavor they so enriched Punjabi language and literature that today Punjabi literature is not inferior in any way to literature in other Indian languages."

The Bible set modern India on its current path to progress by delivering it from its paralysing fatalism. Let's examine that next.

Chapter 3

The Bible Explodes Indian Fatalism
Can stagnant cultures progress?

The fatalism and corruption that enslaved Indian culture were well-portrayed by the great nationalist novelist, Premchand, born Dhanpat Rai Srivastava (1880–1936). Here is one of his descriptions of our pessimistic culture in his classic, *Godaan* (Donation of Cow):

> *They all suffered. The peasant moved about, worked, wept, and put up with oppression without a murmur, as if to suffer was part of his destiny. He had neither hope nor great joy, as if the wellsprings of his life had permanently dried up. He saw no future ahead of him; his sensibility had incurably dulled. Heaps of garbage lay near his door, exuding stench; he neither saw nor was offended. He ate without relish, like a machine gulping down coal; anything that stuffed his belly was good enough for him. He would turn dishonest for a pice [penny] and fight for a handful of grain; his degradation was so terribly complete that he often made no distinction between shame and honour.*

Dhanpat Rai published his early stories under the pen name "Nawab Rai." Later, he changed his pen name to Premchand. He graduated from my alma mater, the University of Allahabad, in 1919. He wrote his stories and novels in Urdu and Hindi, both standardised as literary languages by Bible translators: Urdu by Rev. Henry Martyn (1781-1812) in Kanpur (1808) and Hindi by Rev. Samuel Kellogg (1839-99) in Allahabad (1876). Both Urdu and Hindi grew out of *Hindustani*, created by Scottish surgeon John Borthwick Gilchrist (1749-1841).

In February 1921, Premchand was serving the British government as a Deputy Inspector of Schools. He resigned in response to Mahatma Gandhi's strategy of "Non-Cooperation" to gain India's independence. After quitting his government job, Premchand devoted himself to writing and publishing.

Muslims ruled Delhi from 1192–1857. During those seven centuries, Muslim rulers patronised arts, music, and architecture. They built great monuments such as the Taj Mahal. But they did not build a single institution of higher education where a Gandhi or a Premchand could be trained. Hindu gurus built ashrams and temples in many parts of India, but none of those ashrams or gurukuls grew into a university. Taxila and Nalanda, the great centers of learning in ancient India, were both Buddhist.

During the centuries that Islam ruled much of South Asia, Indian fatalism could not produce a single Gandhi, Tagore, Nehru, Ambedkar, or Premchand. Gautama Buddha's First Noble Truth: *"Life is suffering"* encapsulated our fatalistic thinking. The belief implied that it is futile to expect life without suffering. It offered Nirvana, or cessation of existence, as the only way to escape suffering. Brahmins taught that gods and goddesses could help, but only by extracting appeasements from devotees. If deities t did not receive their bribes, they became inauspicious and harassed good people, creating all sorts of obstacles in a devotee's path.

In contrast, the Bible introduced the Jewish God to India. He was the Saviour God who delivered Hebrews from Egypt's slavery without an 1857-style armed rebellion. This biblical narrative of political deliverance enabled thoughtful Indians, such as Premchand, to accept Mahatma Gandhi's strategy of non-violence.

Much before hearing Gandhi, Premchand was already inspired by his biblical education. He was using his gift of writing to reform his culture as well as free it from British colonial rule. His earliest story *"Duniya ka Sabse Anmol Ratan"* (The Most Precious Jewel in the World), was published in 1907 in an Urdu magazine, *Zamana,* under his first pen name, Nawab Rai. The story argued that the last drop of blood spent for the freedom of the country would be the most precious jewel in the world.

It took time for the government to discover the identity of this insurrectionist "Nawab Rai. The District Magistrate burned the collection of his stories as "seditious" and warned him, "You are lucky that this is the British rule. Had it been the Mughals, both your hands would have been cut off. Your stories are one-sided, and you have committed contempt against the British government."

In order to understand Premchand's love for freedom and his mission to inspire his readers with optimistic nationalism, one has to understand the Bible. German reformer Martin Luther was the first European scholar to see the Bible's idea of politics as a pursuit of freedom. In 1520, it inspired him to write *A Treatise Concerning Christian Liberty*.

In contrast to Luther, Italian diplomat Machiavelli's *The Prince* (1532) saw politics as pursuit of power. After 1575, French philosopher Jean Bodin (1530–1596) began secularising Luther's biblical theology of liberty. That process of pirating the Bible's theology of freedom misled French thinkers such as Jean Jacques Rousseau (1712-1778) and the French revolutionaries (1789-99) to assume that humanist revolutions can bring liberty, equality, and fraternity without God. The French Revolution became a terrible Reign of Terror, ending in the dictatorship of Napoleon Bonaparte.

Premchand's younger contemporary, Dr. Sam Higginbottom (1874–1958), researched rural Allahabad before establishing the Allahabad Agricultural Institute to fight hunger and poverty. His account of my home district agrees with Premchand's:

> As I talked with the villagers around the wells, I was oppressed with a sense of their poverty. From the cradle to the grave, many of them were underfed and undernourished, never knowing what it was to enjoy a good square meal. We suggested that there might be some means of amelioration. But most of them were victims of fatalism. They were sure they were being punished for wrongs they had done in their previous birth, nor did they see how anything could be done about it in this present incarnation. Of what use was it to fight against God? God always got the better of you. The farmers were fa-

talistic, and nothing is more deadly to progress than fatalism, for it cuts the very nerve of all effort.

Our sages had gone beyond the theories of karma and reincarnation in their attempt to philosophise fatalism. They pictured the cosmos as an endless cycle. Each cosmic cycle begins with *Sat Yuga* (Golden Age of Truth) and degenerates into *Treta* (or *Krita*) *Yuga*, to be followed by *Dwapar* and *Kali* (Dark) *Yuga*. The cycle is destroyed at the end of Kali Yuga (Dark Age) to restart a new Sat Yuga (Truth Age). There are hundreds of millions of deities, but none of them can reverse the downward degeneration of the predetermined cosmic order. Even the highest god is incapable of bringing *Achhe Din* (good days) in Kali Yuga (Dark Age).

A fatalistic worldview cannot fight corruption because it believes that the future is predetermined to go from bad to worse. Even gods are impotent to change the downward, destructive direction of the cosmic cycle. This is an important reason why societal corruption, such as bribery, has been India's chronic problem. India's governance began to improve only in the early 1800s, because of the Bible that resisted the corruption of British officials. The Bible became a textbook to prepare the minds and character of young men to govern India at Haileybury College in Hertfordshire (UK), Addiscombe Military Seminary in Surrey (UK), and Fort William College in Calcutta.

The teachers and pundits hired to teach civil servants at Fort William translated the Bible into Indian languages. These translations were then printed at the Mission Press in Serampore. Aspiring civil servants, police officers, judges, and military leaders studied the vernacular Bibles to learn Indian languages and also to understand how God desires nations to be governed.

Charles Grant: The Prophet of India's Renaissance

The Scotsman Charles Grant (1746-1823), a civil servant who rose through the ranks of the British East India Company over his 22 years of employment, became a follower of Christ in Bengal. Studying the Bible convinced him that the British misrule of Bengal could be reformed. In 1786, he appealed to revivalist John Wesley, the founder of

Methodism and England's most respected spiritual leader, to send missionaries to educate and transform Bengal.

In Grant and Wesley's time education was not regarded as commerce. The Bible had portrayed education as the Church's mission to train nations in intellectual truth, personal godliness, and practical skills necessary to steward the earth. Wesley's Director for missions expressed their unwillingness to partner with a Company steeped in corruption.

Disappointed, on 17 September 1787, Grant sent an expanded version of his appeal to fourteen Christian leaders in England. The only person to see Grant's appeal as consistent with God's mandate was Charles Simeon in Cambridge. An influential preacher, Simeon was the priest of the Holy Trinity Church and a fellow of King's College. He began motivating Christian students at Cambridge University such as Henry Martyn and Claudius Buchanan to prepare themselves to serve God in India.

In 1792, a prominent Evangelical Member of Parliament, William Wilberforce (1759-1833), teamed up with Charles Grant. Wilberforce had been waging a relentless war against Britain's lucrative trade in African slaves.

When the East India Company's Charter came up for renewal in 1793, Wilberforce presented Grant's case that it was immoral to leave India to the mercy of traders and soldiers: Parliament must allow educators to go to India to spread the light of truth. Wilberforce won the vote in the House of Commons but lost it in the House of Lords. Too many Lords owned stocks in the two companies that were exploiting Africa and India. They did not want missionaries to report on their misgovernance. This is the reason Charles Simeon's proteges could not come as "missionaries." They had to be smuggled into India as "chaplains" to the East India Company.

From 1793 to 1813, for 20 years, Wilberforce continued his battle for India's transformation. He persisted because he knew that the Bible commands God's servants to illuminate every nation with the light of truth. His effort was strengthened when Charles Grant rose to become a Member of Parliament, a Director, and eventually the Chairman of the East India Company.

The political success had to wait until 1813, when the East India Company's charter came up for renewal. The Parliament supported Wilberforce and Grant and required the Company to spend Rupees 100,000 from its profits for public education in India. Why was a capitalistic, commercial company required to educate and develop Britain's subjects?

It is not a trader's business to educate the poor. Nor did Hindu, Muslim, or British rulers see education as their responsibility. In contrast, the Church took on this responsibility in Western Europe because the Bible taught that God desires for all people to be saved from their sin and come to the knowledge of the truth (1 Timothy 2:4). It also declared that the Church was created to be the pillar and the foundation of the truth (1 Timothy 3:15). Governments that honoured God's word supported the Church's mission to educate.

For the Church, education was inseparable from character formation. Sin had corrupted God's image in man; and salvation included reforming God's holy image in men and women.

Moral education was understood as the key to building great nation because God Himself had declared,

"Abraham will surely become a great and powerful nation, and all nations on earth will be blessed through him. For I have chosen him, so that he will direct his children and his household after him to keep the way of the Lord by doing what is right and just, so that the Lord will bring about for Abraham what he has promised him." (Genesis 18: 18-19)

Four centuries after Abraham, Moses reminded liberated slaves that obeying God's law was the secret of becoming a wise and great nation,

"See, I have taught you decrees and laws as the Lord my God commanded me, so that you may follow them in the land you are entering to take possession of it. Observe them carefully, for this will show your wisdom and understanding to the nations, who will hear about all these decrees and say, "Surely this great nation is a wise and understanding people." What other nation is so great as to have their gods near them the way the Lord our God is near us whenever we

pray to him? And what other nation is so great as to have such righteous decrees and laws as this body of laws I am setting before you today?" (Deuteronomy 4: 5-8)

The British Parliament required the East India Company to use a part of its profits for public education because the Lord Jesus commissioned his disciples to teach the whole truth to all the nations of the world. (Matthew 28:18–20). That's why the education clause in the 1813 Charter was called "the missionary clause." It required the East India Company to allow missionary-educators to come to India under license. At that time, "secular" education did not exist; only missionaries had the motivation to leave their homes to go and build nations via education.

Like most young Englishmen, Charles Grant came to India as a penniless and non-religious (secular) individual in 1767 to make money for himself. He witnessed the rampant corruption in the Company as well as among Indians. He also witnessed the catastrophic famine of 1769–70, that claimed the lives of over ten million (one crore) people. That devastation deeply troubled Grant. Famines occurred periodically, but ignorance about hygiene, nutrition, and disease killed people every day. Two factors prevented the progress of agriculture and food production: first, the absence of science and technology, and second, the lack of just and responsible governance.

He discovered how unscrupulous pundits, astrologers, and sorcerers fueled myths and superstitions to prey on the meager earnings of impoverished peasants. He saw a religious culture that sanctified the killing of newborn girls, the burning alive of young widows, and the abandonment of elderly widows left to starve on the streets of India's so-called holy cities. Grant realised that the mercantile interests of a merciless Company made it too callous to manage natural calamities or to reform the inhumanity of South Asian religiosity.

The death of his two children within a week forced Grant to come to terms with fundamental religious questions about the meaning and purpose of life: If death is the end of our lives, then does it matter how we live and treat others? What is life? Does the human soul continue beyond death? What happens after death?

Grant knew that he was a sinner. If God were to judge humanity, he too would face punishment. The Bible taught that God had created Adam and Eve for eternal life, but sin introduced physical death. Worse still, its ultimate consequence was eternal separation from God—hell. This realisation drew him to the *Good News*: that Jesus Christ had taken human sin and its penalty upon Himself on the cross. Sinless and pure, Jesus died as the Lamb of God—the divine sacrifice for humanity's redemption. Grant learned that through repentance and accepting Jesus as his Savior and Lord, he could receive forgiveness, reconciliation with God, and eternal life. In 1776, following his wife's example, he turned to God for mercy and the forgiveness of his sins.

Though nominally already a Christian, Grant's authentic spiritual conversion transformed everything about him. He joined a small group of men who gathered regularly for Bible study and prayer, seeking to live by God's Word. The Bible commanded him to love his neighbors as himself and to be a light in the darkness that surrounded him. This conviction ignited his passion to serve Indian society, which was being devastated both by the corrupt religiosity of Brahminism and by the ruthless secular greed of his own Company.

Charles Grant returned to England in 1790, disappointed that his appeal for missionaries seemed to have gone unheeded. Wilberforce, who knew that biblical spirituality involves patience and perseverance, encouraged Grant to write out his rationale for missions. That resulted in the first systematic presentation of the need to reform India through education. His book had a long title, *Observations on the State of Society among the Asiatic Subjects of Great Britain, particularly with respect to Morals and the Means of Improving It. Written chiefly in the year 1792.*

It was divine providence that William Carey also published his book, *An Inquiry into the Obligation of Christians to Use Means for the Conversion of the Heathen*, in 1792. While Grant's book was written to influence the British Parliament; Carey's was written to mobilise the church. When Grant and Wilberforce began championing India's cause in Parliament, Carey and his associates started laying the groundwork for modern vernacular/moral education in India.

Carey's associates Joshua and Hannah Marshman began schools and started Asia's first vernacular college in Serampore in 1818. Later, Carey, the mission's leader, taught half of each week at Serampore and the rest at Calcutta's Fort William College, which was born as a result of Grant and Wilberforce's efforts in Parliament. One of history's greatest linguists and Bible translators, Carey became a model for countless missionary educators, beginning with those sent by Grant and Simeon.

Besides translating the Bible, Carey regularly lectured on science and astronomy, which he believed were aspects of the Bible's worldview. For the same reason Carey taught astronomy, botany, gardening, forestry, and agriculture as a practitioner-writer. It was Carey's influence on reformers like Raja Ram Mohan Roy (1772-1833) that triggered what is called India's Renaissance.

Charles Grant's argument—that the light of education in truth was the cure for India's intellectual, moral, and religious darkness—influenced Parliament's 1793 debate on the Company's charter. Until 1797, his book was hand-copied and distributed. Eventually, the British government recognised it as the best available study of the misery of the average Indian, a misery which had been compounded by the Company's misrule. In 1812, the Parliament ordered Grant's *Observations* to be published as a state paper.

No one objected to Grant's case for education as a mission because the Humanists had no organisation, nor any interest in educating the poor. As mentioned earlier, education was not considered the responsibility of the state. Education of the next generation fell under the auspices of the Church, even if funds came from the state or private philanthropists. Grant's passionate yet well-informed arguments triggered the educational movement that enabled India to become one of the world's leading centers for education.

Grant's position as the Company's Director enabled him to send Simeon's Cambridge proteges as chaplains for the Company to India. This group of dedicated scholars which included men such as Henry Martyn and Claudius Buchanan, did not limit themselves to serving Europeans. They followed William Carey's mission to turn Indian dialects into literary languages by translating the Bible into the vernaculars, i.e., the spoken, non-classical languages of the common man.

Younger missionaries such as Alexander Duff built upon their work to bring higher education to India. They trained and encouraged Indian writers to write in vernaculars. The development of vernaculars such as Bengali, Urdu, Hindustani, Marathi, Tamil, Telugu, Malayalam, and Gujarati became the most important key for mass education.

Missionary-reformers taught Indian social reformers such as Raja Ram Mohan Roy (1772–1833), Mahatma Jotiba Phule (1827–90), and Dr Bhimrao Ambedkar (1891–1956) the secret of the unique development of Christian nations. That began with the development of vernaculars into vibrant literary languages, wholesome literature, and education that sought truth, cultivated character, honed skills, and sparked a passion for nation-building. Inspired by the Bible, Indian reformers made great sacrifices to educate themselves. They promoted education (not the purchase of degrees) as the most important need of the downtrodden.

Along with his wife, Savitribai, Jotiba Phule became the first low-caste Indian to follow the missionaries' example. He educated Shudras and the untouchables. The Shudras (manual labourers) occupied the lowest rung of the four-tier castesystem. They were placed below the Brahmins (priests), the Kshatriya (rulers), and the Vaishya (businessmen/money lenders). At the time, the Untouchables were considered too degraded even to be included in the four-fold caste system.

Since Independence, Indian bureaucracy, politics, and business have become increasingly corrupt. One significant reason is that non-biblical rationalist education has shown itself to be incapable of cultivating ethical character. Before Independence, missionary education embedded the Bible in school curricula, producing virtues that are now rapidly vanishing—one of them being *Truth*.

Pandit Madan Mohan Malviya (1861–1946), who studied in Allahabad before founding Banaras Hindu University, also served as President of the Indian National Congress and established *Satya Mev Jayate* ("Truth Alone Triumphs") as its motto. Eventually, *Satya Mev Jayate* became India's national motto. Building a nation on truth in place of myths was a consequence of an education based on the Bible's emphasis on truth. Rejecting myths began to weaken the caste system's stranglehold over Indian society. The idea that all men are created equal is not an observable, scientific truth but a scriptural revelation. The first wave of missionaries, such as Ziegenbalg and Carey, brought this truth to India. Later missionaries educated Jotiba Phule and Bhimrao Ambedkar to ensure that this truth would transform Indian culture.

This truth, loved by the Bahujan (the majority people, especially the lower castes), is revealed exclusively in the Bible. Traditional Buddhism rejected the Hindu idea that God created castes from different parts of his body, but it agreed with Hinduism that people are born unequal due to their karma in previous lives. The assertion that Buddha taught human equality is a modern myth fabricated by thinkers who came many centuries after him, such as Rabindranath Tagore. In his dance-drama, *Chandalika*, Tagore took the incident of Jesus' encounter with an "untouchable" Samaritan woman, recorded in the 4th chapter of John, and replace Christ with a Buddhist monk.

Bible-based missionary education didn't just impart information and skills—it made character development equally essential. This is precisely what shaped the politicians, civil and military servants, lawyers, and judges of independent India into individuals of extraordinary integrity and caliber. In stark contrast, post-Independence education, which discarded the Bible, has fueled India's descent into corruption. It has tainted not only the upper-caste elite but also the very Bahujan leaders, civil servants, and businessmen who once fought for justice and reform.

The Bible kindled hope in a subcontinent enslaved by fatalism. Among the people that for millennia had known only fiefdoms and empires, a Biblically-informed education implanted the idea of "nation." A people who formerly claimed allegiance only to their caste and tribe began to cultivate "nationalism" as a value.

Modern education without the Bible's moral compass produces black marketeers who cheat their nation, loot public funds, and evade taxes. By contrast, the Bible has a record of reforming British rule and giving India honourable civil servants, principled police, and impartial judiciary. The next chapter will chronicle that history.

Chapter 4

The Bible Reformed the British Raj[2]

Sardar Vallabhbhai Patel (1875–1955), India's first Deputy Prime Minister and Home Minister, described the colonial Civil Services as "The Steel Frame of India."

Who or what built that frame?

The short answer is: the Bible.

Between 1765 to 1820, British rulers were as corrupt as today's Indian civil servants. Most Indians feel that our criminal politicians use civil servants to loot our tax money and extract bribes from helpless citizens. Now they are also using the police to persecute political opponents and religious minorities. Why then did Patel, India's "Iron Man," describe colonial-era civil services as the "steel frame" of justice and fairness that held India together?

Vallabhbhai Patel, who fought against the British Raj, praised civil servants on 21 April 1947 at Metcalf House in Delhi. He argued that after independence, the Indian Civil Services (ICS), created by colonial rulers, should continue serving the new nation. Its name would change from ICS to IAS (Indian Administrative Services). Patel's phrase "the steel frame" came from a 1922 speech by British Prime Minister David Lloyd George.

---

2. This chapter was written with help from Samuel Davidson.

Management guru Peter Drucker described colonial civil services as a model of public administration and management. It was the reason, he asserted, that colonialism survived for two centuries. Many of its cadre were sons of British pastors. Their parents and churches prayed that these young men would serve India with diligence and integrity. Their prayers were answered.

Drucker does not defend colonialism. He knew that the British Raj was marked by muddled policies, indecision, misdirection, and failures. It survived for as long as it did because the Bible-based Evangelical movement built the Indian Civil Services. The ICS, says Drucker, was Britain's "supreme administrative accomplishment":

> [The Civil Servants] *were younger sons of poor country parsons*, with no prospects at home and little standing in English society. Their pay was low, and such opportunities for loot or gain as their predecessors had enjoyed in the swashbuckling days of the East India Company a hundred years earlier had, by 1860, been completely eliminated by both law and custom. These untrained, not very bright, and totally inexperienced youngsters ran districts comparable in size and population to small European countries. And they ran them practically all by themselves with a minimum of direction and supervision from the top. Some, of course, became casualties and broke under the strain, falling victim to alcohol, to native women, or—the greatest danger of them all—to sloth. But most of them did what they were expected to do and did it reasonably well. They gave India, for the first time in its long and tragic history, peace, a measure of freedom from famine, and a little security of life, worship, and property. *They administered justice impartially and, at least as far as they themselves were concerned, honestly and without corruption. They collected taxes by and large, impartially and equitably.* They did not make policy, and in the end they foundered because they had none. But they administered, and administered well.[3]

Robert Clive, a clerk in the Madras office of the East India Company, laid the foundations of the British Raj in 1757 by defeating Bengal's

---

3. Peter Drucker. *Management: Tasks, Responsibilities, Practices*, pp. 403-404. Emphasis added.

Nawab, Siraj-ud-Daulah. Clive supported the appointment of the new Nawab, Mir Qasim, who ruled until 1763. In 1762, Mir Qasim described British corruption in a letter to the Governor and his Council,

> And this is the way your gentlemen behave; they make a disturbance all over my country, plunder the people, injure and disgrace my servants... They forcibly take away the goods and commodities of the peasants, merchants, etc., for the fourth part of their value, and by ways of violence and oppressions they oblige the peasants to give five rupees for goods which are worth but one rupee.[4]

As mentioned earlier, seven decades later, one of Britain's greatest historians, Lord Macaulay, confirmed Mir Qasim's testimony regarding the corruption of British rulers. In his *Essay on Clive*, Macaulay wrote that the British East India Company was a "gang of public robbers" that "had spread terror through[out] the whole plain of Bengal." Its governance was as "oppressive as the most oppressive form of barbarian despotism... strong with all the [military] strength of civilisation. It resembled the government of evil Genii rather than the government of human tyrants."

The British Parliament denounced Clive as a corrupt "Nabob." He was followed by Governor General Warren Hastings, who expanded British rule in India. Hastings too, was tried for corruption. During his trial, Edmund Burke, the father of modern conservatism, put his finger on the root of a philosophical problem. Accusing the British East India Company, Burke said,

> "... these Gentlemen have formed a plan of Geographical morality, by which the duties of men in public and private situations are not to be governed by their relations to the Great Governor of the Universe or by their relations to men, but by climates, degrees of longitude, and latitude.... As if, when you have crossed the equinoctial line, all the virtues die... as if there were a kind of baptism, like that practiced by seamen, by which they unbaptise themselves of all that they learned in Europe and commence a new order and system of things."

---

4. Philip Mason. *The Men Who Ruled India.* pp. 38-39.

Burke's charge was that in India, a corrupt East India Company was practicing a 'Geographical' or relative morality that was not governed by God's moral (absolute) laws. In his influential work, *The Men Who Ruled India,* Philip Mason points out that this moral relativism was justified to maintain British rule and trade in India. Trade interests overruled God's moral law.

The Company presumed that "to be fair to Indians was to be prejudiced against the English."

Burke's accusation, confirmed by Charles Grant and others, inspired British Evangelicals to reform the Company. Anglican Evangelicals were just beginning to emerge out of the Wesleyan revival of the late eighteenth century. They were called "Evangelicals" because they had individually repented of their sins and asked the Lord Jesus Christ to become their Savior. They were moral rebels, now reconciled to their Heavenly Father, dedicated to ensuring that God's will was done in their lives and in his world. Historian Ian Bradley explains their worldview and mission in his book *A Call to Seriousness: The Evangelical Impact on the Victorians:*

> The great obstacle to missionary endeavour in India at the beginning of the nineteenth century arose from the East India Company's conviction that missionaries would only excite the natives and disturb its profitable trading activities. Because of this, it refused them entry to the subcontinent. In this situation, there was only one thing for the Evangelicals to do if they wanted to secure the triumph of vital religion in India, and that was to infiltrate the higher echelons of the Company themselves so that they could change its policy. Their takeover of the Company's directorate in the early nineteenth century was spectacular: there was no year between 1807 and 1830 when either the Chairman or the Deputy Chairman of the Board of Directors was not an Evangelical.[5]

Charles Simeon, the Anglican priest in Cambridge mentioned earlier, is considered the Father of British Evangelicalism. His response to the East India Company's corruption was to mentor Cambridge

---

5. Ian Bradley, "Mission to the Heathen," in *A Call to Seriousness,* p. 74.

students to go to India as missionaries. They had to be smuggled into India as undercover missionaries because, in 1793, the British Parliament had rejected the Evangelical Bill to allow missionary-educators into Bengal.

Rev. Claudius Buchanan, one of Simeon's well-known proteges, shared the evangelical conviction that British rule in India was not an accident of history but God's providential act. Buchanan took up the challenge to reform the Company by training the young men who governed India as the Company's civil, police, and judicial servants. They needed to know Indian languages and be trained spiritually and intellectually to know God's will and put it above their self-interest and the Company's profits.

Edmund Burke had already lamented that the Company was sending to India the riffraff of British society. They had nothing to gain by remaining in Britain and much to gain by looting India, if they could survive the climate and tropical diseases. Buchanan decided to challenge Christians to send their sons to govern India with integrity. He organised essay-writing competitions in seven Irish, Scottish, and English universities and colleges on the topic of, "How can Britain give good governance to India?"

As a Cambridge student, Thomas Babbington Macaulay was one of the winners of these competitions. He is famous for his 1835 *Minute on Education and* as the creator of the India Penal Code. During 1852–56, Macaulay played important roles in laying the foundations of the university movement in India, opening the doors for Indians to become civil servants, and ensuring that civil servants were recruited strictly on merit and not because of nepotism or bribes.

Transforming the moral character of the Company's governance required Rev. Buchanan to make an important intellectual contribution. In 1805, he challenged the idea that separation of Church and State means separating business and governance from God's moral law. His "*Memoir on the expediency of an ecclesiastical establishment for British India; both as the means of perpetuating the Christian religion among our own countrymen; and as a foundation for the ultimate civilisation of the natives,*" provided the intellectual basis for the evangelical engagement with Bengal's governance. The first part of Buchanan's *Memoir* dealt with the degenerating morality of British rule in India and emphasised the need for a formal Anglican presence to minister to the Europeans in India.

Charles Grant had already emphasised the need for reforming the Company's morality in his 1792 book, *Observations on the State of Society Among the Asiatic Subjects of Great Britain*. Buchanan offered practical suggestions on how to do it. His case was strongly supported by Lord Teignmouth through his *Considerations on the Practicability, Policy, and Obligation of Communicating to the Natives of India the Knowledge of Christianity*. Their books exposed the hollow prejudice of critics who claimed that missionary-minded evangelicals were religious fanatics who should not intervene in politics. Readers were able to see that the evangelicals had a better conception of the British Empire, in which the ruler and the ruled interacted beyond mere commercialism. Christians viewed the Indo-British relationship in the light of the Bible's teaching on the covenant between government and those being governed. Their relationship was providential, bound by mutual moral obligations. Relativistic 'geographical' morality needed to be replaced by godly governance. God's "Ten Commandments had no purely localised application." They were binding upon the Company, which could not be allowed to remain a gang of public robbers. (See Mayhew, 25.)

Thomas Gisborne, an Anglican priest and a member of the evangelical "Clapham Sect," went further in challenging the entitlement mentality that pervaded the services. He wrote what became a textbook for civil servants, *Enquiries into the Duties of Men*, first published in 1795. It was a handbook for men who aspired to various callings: pastor, politician, civil servant, armed personnel, lawyer, doctor, tradesman, etc. In his chapter *"On the Duties of the Executive Officers of Government,"* he gave a detailed treatment of the moral composition that ought to constitute a civil servant and his behavior in various eventualities that may arise in his career.

Civil servants such as Sir James Stephen lived out these duties. His father, also named James Stephen, was also a member of the Clapham

Sect. Ian Bradley writes about his impact upon the British idea of Civil Service:

> "It was he who created the two grades of mechanical and intellectual in the Civil Service and who formulated the modern concept of civil servants as anonymous purveyors of impartial and expert advice to ministers. *'You stand not in need of statesmen in disguise,'* he told the Royal Commission on the Civil Service in 1854, *'but of intelligent, steady, methodical men of business.'*"[6]

Claudius Buchanan served as the Vice Provost of Calcutta's Fort WilliamCollege, which had been founded in order to educate the officers of the Secretariat. For three years the young men studied Indian history, law, oriental languages, ethics, international law, and general history. Its education system was modeled along the lines of Oxford and Cambridge. It was not a commercial school that taught the art of governing. Its statutes were recorded by Andrew Mayhew, who served as the Director of Public Instruction in the Central Provinces of India. The Biblical worldview insisted that the living God governs the cosmos. Human governance in turn was God's "Sacred Trust" given to his children whom he had called for that vocation.

This Bible-inspired idea of trusteeship continued to shape the mindset, even of Mahatma Gandhi's generation a century and a half later. Mayhew writes,

> "...the civil servants of the Company, no longer 'the agents of a commercial concern' but guardians of 'a sacred trust,' were to study the people and its languages, improve their morals, and fortify their minds (by science and the classics). Here they would be 'guarded against temptation and corruption with which the nature of the climate and the peculiar depravity of the people of India will assail them.' Then and then only will they learn 'to diffuse affluence, happiness, willing obedience, and grateful attachment over every district.'"

The aspiring young civil servants were schooled in these reforming ideas at Haileybury College outside of London.

---

6. Ian Bradley, "Serious Callings" in *A Call to Seriousness*, p. 163.

Historian Ian Bradley explains who these young men were:
"The civil servants of the latter part of the nineteenth century were predominantly from the middle class and often from Evangelical backgrounds. They had been brought up at home and at school to the discipline of hard work and regularity. They regarded their job as a vocation. For them, public service was not simply a source of personal gratification or gain; it was a matter of absolute moral duty. In fashioning this ethic of public service which made the British administration the envy of the world, the Evangelicals had played no small part."[7]

Evangelical leadership in education made it much more than training in leadership skills. It refined the character and cultivated personal integrity. These servants became very different from the British rulers in the eighteenth century. They began to be noticed as men of upright conduct and benefactors of the public. They were not feared for brutality but revered for their intolerance for corruption, for upholding the rule of law over the autocratic dispensation of power at the hands of rulers, for being concerned about matters of justice and mercy, and for successfully installing an infrastructure for the benefit of the governed. They did more than create the "steel frame" that sustained India after Independence. After various Indian attempts failed to write a Constitution for India—e.g., "The Commonwealth of India" Bill of 1925 and the Motilal Nehru Committee's draft of 1928—it was British civil servants who drafted the India Act of 1935. That became the basis for independent India's Constitution adopted in 1950.

What reformed a corrupt Company? The straight answer is—the Bible. British civil servants had to govern a vast, illiterate populace who did not speak Sanskrit, Arabic, or Persian. They spoke vernaculars which had no grammar, textbooks or literature. How could civil servants themselves learn the languages of the people they were called to serve?

The college used the vernacular Bible to teach officers Indian languages. For this reason, Fort William College in Calcutta became the initial center for Bible translation. Missionary linguists such as William

---

7. Ian Bradley, "Serious Callings" in *A Call to Seriousness*, p. 163.

Carey teamed up with Pundits to translate the Bible into Indian languages. Later, the responsibility for translating Bibles was handed over to the British and Foreign Bible Society. Most of these vernacular Bibles were printed at the Serampore Mission Press. Aspiring civil servants studied those Bibles to learn Indian languages and also how God wanted nations to be governed.

Chapter 5

The Bible
and Women's Liberation[8]

At the southernmost tip of India in the city of Nagercoil, an eight-year-old girl was found lying on the ground, famished, almost dead. Her body had been brutalised. People who passed by saw her but abandoned her to her fate. Why meddle in someone else's karma and court trouble?

Thankfully, Charles Mead (1792-1873), a member of the London Missionary Society, was compassionate and naive enough to intervene. He picked her up, fed her, and began the treatment to revive her. When she was able to talk, the missionary learnt that she was running away from her slave master because she could no longer bear his brutalities. She pleaded with Rev. Mead not to hand her back to her master but to keep her in his home.

The slave master found out that his property was at Charles Mead's residence. He came fuming and ranting, demanding that his slave be returned. Rev. Mead tried hard to dissuade him, negotiate a ransom price, and plead with his conscience. The little girl hid behind the door, trembling at her owner's angry voice. The master refused to listen to the pleas of mercy and compassion. He did not want money; he wanted his slave.

The British never colonised the southern tip of India. It was a Hindu kingdom, ruled by the kings of Travancore. Slavery was legal, and

---
8. I am grateful for Prof. Mercia Justin's assistance for this chapter.

Rev. Mead was bound by the law of the land. Hindu culture compelled Mead to let the master take back his property. The pain of seeing a helpless young girl go back into slavery changed Mead's soul. The Spirit of Christ and his study of the Bible inspired him to become an agent of India's transformation. The God who had liberated the Hebrews from Egypt's slavery was able to emancipate Indian slaves, making them free citizens.

Empire and Nation: Slavery and Freedom

An empire's expansion depends upon its military prowess and brutality, but a nation progresses by empowering its women. Moses' life vindicated the proverb, "The hand that rocks the cradle rules the world." An Egyptian princess rescued the Hebrew infant Moses from the Nile River and, following his sister's advice, hired Moses' own mother to nurse him. His mother, it would seem, prepared Moses to identify with his own people and become someone God could use to transform slaves into a great nation.

India's Modern Women

How did India become one of the world's first major democracies to choose a woman in 1966 as its Prime Minister, Mrs. Indira Gandhi? Great Britain followed in 1979, making Margaret Thatcher its first female prime minister. Germany elected Angela Merkel as its first female Chancellor much later, in 2005. The USA, the birthplace of the women's liberation movement, is still waiting for a female president. The Bible was the force to emancipate Indian women.

India has a long way to go to achieve respectable levels of gender equality. Yet it was the Bible that started India's journey in the direction of liberating and empowering women. The Bible triggered a series of intellectual and political battles to rescue women from female infanticide, forced illiteracy, child marriage, *purdah* (veil), widow burning (*sati*), *devadasi* (temple prostitution), forced immodesty, dowry, polygamy, and abandonment through *Sannyas* and *Brahmacharya*. Each of these battles began because of the Bible's unique revelation of male and female equality, since both are created equally in the image of God.

The *inequality* of men and women is an observable fact. Hinduism and Buddhism explain it by theories of karma and reincarnation. A soul is born a female because of her bad karma in previous lives. The Bible, on the other hand, explained the female's subjugation through its doctrine of sin. It offered salvation because the Lamb of God took human sin and its curse upon Calvary's cross. Redemption includes restoration of God's original design and purpose for men and women. This redemption erases, rather than institutionalises, inequality between the sexes.

Explanations for this inequality as well as justifications for the status quo were offered by the doctrines of karma and reincarnation, but were problematic at the popular level. Seekers of "spiritual enlightenment" abandoned their wives for philosophical reasons. The idea that everything is one means that male-female dualism is an illusion—Maya. Adherence to Monism or Vedanta required men, including Mahatma Gandhi, to abandon their wives, making them *de facto* widows. We will return to this philosophical dehumanisation after considering some of the specific battles that liberated Indian women.

Female Infanticide

Not every girl conceived in her mother's womb sees the outside world. As recent as 2023, the sex ratio in rural India was 985 women to 1000 men. The global average ratio is 1030 women to 1000 men. Female infanticide was a socially accepted practice. Advances in medical technology have made it easier to murder female babies before they are born.

In my earlier books such as *The Book That Made Your World*, I have described some of the battles Ruth and I fought to save newborn girls in central India. It was hard to believe that killing newborn girls was a socially approved practice. Many parents, not just the impoverished class, felt that one daughter was enough to cook, clean, and look after her siblings. The second daughter was an unnecessary liability. Our religious culture adorned infanticide with religious garb. Female infanticide was portrayed as sacrificing to the river goddess the fruit of one's body—a daughter—to wash away the sin of one's soul.

Such rituals, deemed "sacred" in Hinduism, violated the command of the God of the Bible: "You shall not kill." Through the tireless efforts of Christian missionaries such as William Carey in Calcutta, the East India Company banned the murder of infant girls in the Bengal Regulatory Act XXI of 1795. The Regulating Act of 1804 and the Female Infanticide Act of 1870 went on to criminalise these socio-religious customs.

Child Marriage and Polygamy

Rampant sexual immorality made child marriage a social necessity. Unless they were married off before puberty, most girls were likely to get pregnant against their wishes. Who then would marry them?

If the adult husband died, the little girl became an unmarriageable widow. No Hindu, Muslim, Sikh, or Buddhist ruler ever took a census of child marriages or child widows. The last census of the nineteenth century in British-ruled Bengal revealed that in and around Calcutta, there were ten thousand widows under the age of four, and over fifty thousand widows between the ages of five and nine.

Child marriage robbed girls of the opportunity to study and develop. Becoming a widow condemned them to a future without income, security, dignity, and purpose. If they did not want to be slaves in their in-laws' homes, then one of their few remaining options was temple prostitution. Religion, however, added insult to a widow's injury. It taught that her widowhood and suffering were proof of bad karma in her previous life and justly earned.

It was standard practice for both Hindu and Muslim aristocrats to take multiple wives. Thus, no ruler or religious leader considered banning the practices of child marriage or polygamy. The high-caste social reformer Raja Ram Mohan Roy himself was married to three wives: first at the age of 9 (in 1781), then at 10 (in 1782), and again at 21 (in 1793). His first wife died young. The second wife lived as his wife for 29 years after his third marriage. Hinduism had no concept of divorce because a wife was primarily a piece of her husband's property. Religion promoted polygamy: Krishna, the preacher of Bhagavad Gita, was said to have married more than 14,000 wives. His best-known consort, Radha, was not his wife.

Only in the 1850s did Hindu reformers begin to promote the biblical idea of monogamy. One of the first such writers was Ishwar Chandra Vidhyasagar (1820–1891). He taught Sanskrit at Fort William College, in the process becoming personally acquainted with Christian missionaries and civil servants. This interaction helped him appreciate the revolutionary ideas that Hindu women and men could be empowered by permitting widows to remarry and that a man ought only to have one wife. That one wife deserved to be loved, and not abandoned. Until the 1850s, it had only been the Christian missionaries who had emphasised monogamy.

Gradually, other Indians began to agree that marrying more than one wife degrades women and weakens children, husbands, and communities. A wife as a man's property could be gambled away, as in the case of Draupadi in the *Mahabharata*. Some husbands—including the ideal man, Rama—abandoned their wives for social (non-philosophical) reasons. Others, such as Mahatma Gandhi, abandoned their wives for philosophical reasons. Their pursuit of divinity, as we shall see, required Sannyas/Brahmacharya and sexual (Tantric) mysticism. These "religious" reasons justified a guru's multiple sexual partnerships with male and female devotees.

Keshab Chandra Sen (1838-1884), a crypto-Christian scholar, was the first social reformer to urge British rulers to make polygamy illegal and to raise the minimum age of marriage to 16. This perspective began to gain ground partly due to the fact that in 1857, an outnumbered East India Company had overcome a major military revolt by Indian soldiers. This defeat forced thoughtful Indians to seek out the secret of superior British strength. Some, including Sen, began to feel that one factor that made Britain stronger was that an Englishman had only one wife. And that the Bible required him to love his own wife, not his neighbour's. He was required to love her, not merely momentarily, but for the rest of her life! A husband could not divorce her without proper reasons acceptable to the church and to the courts. This understanding of marriage, as a one man-one woman, exclusive and permanent union, made a wife secure. It allowed her to stand up for her own dignity as well as her children's needs and rights. Monogamy did more than empower mothers and children. Strong wives and children made men stronger. Such realisation strengthened the case for banning polygamy.

However, the bloody revolt of 1857 also made British rulers cautious about disturbing India's social traditions. They could not muster up the courage to prohibit polygamy outright. The tradition of Hindu and Muslim elites taking multiple wives persisted as a part of Indian culture.

During the 1920s and 30s, various forums debated the need to reform Hindu marriage in order to empower Hindu women. In 1937, the debate over a Hindu woman's right to family property became particularly fierce. That led to the formation of a Hindu Law Committee in 1941. The committee was unable to resolve the controversy. A new committee was constituted in 1944 with a mandate to frame a bill to codify Hindu law. This new committee submitted its report to the colonial government on February 21, 1947. A year later, on April 9, 1948, Dr. Bhimrao Ambedkar, the low-caste chairman of the committee appointed to draft the Constitution, submitted the Hindu Code Bill to the Constituent Assembly.

The Assembly, however, was dominated by high-caste Hindu politicians who rejected the effort to legally empower Hindu women. The same "freedom fighters" who had fought to liberate India from British colonialism were too weak to fight their own traditions, which had enslaved Hindu women for thousands of years. Their opposition to the Hindu Code Bill forced Pandit Jawaharlal Nehru to advise Dr. Ambedkar to get the Constitution approved without clearly defining the rights of a Hindu woman or Hindu marriage.

The angry and inconclusive debates in the Constituent Assembly forced Dr. Ambedkar to study the cultural and religious enslavement of Indian women. In 1951, as independent India's first Law Minister, he submitted to the Parliament a refined version of the Hindu Code Bill. It included:

- Equal inheritance rights for widows, sons, and daughters
- Prohibition of polygamy for Hindu men
- The right of women to seek divorce
- Legalisation of marriage for widows

- Ending marriages within the same caste

Our first prime minister, Pandit Nehru, was a product of British education himself and a supporter of the bill designed to liberate Indian women. Devout Hindus, on the other hand, led by V. D. Savarkar and the Hindu Mahasabha, opposed the Ambedkar-Nehru Bill. These "high" caste men saw the attempt to reform Hindu marriage and liberate Hindu women as a hideous attempt to bring Hindu society under the Bible's revelation that God created only one Eve for one Adam, and they were made equally in God's image.

Militant Hindus were able to muster serious opposition to the reforms, within as well as outside Parliament, because equality of male and female is not an observable scientific fact. Inequality is a fact. Hindu scriptures enshrined that inequality as a sacred part of their religion. This conflict was the immediate context of the Hindu attack on the Constitution, which had begun several months before the Constitution was approved on November 26, 1949.

Four days later, on November 30, Hindutva's mouthpiece, *The Organiser*, explained,

> *The worst* [thing] *about the new Constitution of Bharat* [India] *is that there is nothing Bharatiya* [Indian] *about it. The drafters of the constitution have incorporated in it elements of British, American, Canadian, Swiss, and sundry other* [Christian] *Constitutions. But there is no trace of ancient Bharatiya constitutional laws, institutions, nomenclature and phraseology in it... in our Constitution, there is no mention of the unique constitutional development in ancient Bharat. Manu's Laws were written long before Lycurgus of Sparta or Solon of Persia. To this day, his laws, as enunciated in the Manusmriti, excite the admiration of the world and elicit spontaneous obedience and conformity. But to our constitutional pundits that means nothing...*
>
> *Manusmriti is that scripture which is most worshipable after Vedas for our Hindu Nation and which, from ancient times, has become the basis of our culture-customs, thought and practice. This book for centuries has codified the spiritual and divine march of our nation. Even today, the rules which are followed by crores of Hindus*

in their lives [marriages] *and practice are based on Manusmriti. Today Manusmriti is Hindu Law.*⁹

Some Hindus from Nehru's own party opposed the bill, meant to liberate Hindu women from millennia of religiously sanctioned enslavement. Our first president, Dr. Rajendra Prasad, hinted that he might veto the bill even if the Parliament voted for it.

Pandit Nehru needed to prepare his ruling party for the 1951–52 elections. He did not want high-caste Hindus to unite Hindu voters against him. It seemed more important to him to defeat the religious outlook that had killed Mahatma Gandhi than to give Hindu women rights over their own lives, property, and husbands. Therefore, Nehru backed out of his support for the Hindu Code Bill. That infuriated Dr. Ambedkar who had invested enormous intellectual and emotional energy to emancipate Indian women. He knew that the code of Manu, *Manusmriti,* was the force that had weakened India by enslaving women and lower castes. He went as far as to publicly burn the *Manusmriti* on December 25, 1927, during the Mahad Satyagraha. In 1946 he wrote, "If Hindu Raj does become a fact, it will, no doubt, be the greatest calamity for this country."¹⁰

Frustrated with his government's unwillingness to reform Hindu marriage, Ambedkar resigned as Nehru's Law Minister. After 105 years of debates and demands, from 1850–1955, the Parliament finally passed a set of laws that mirrored the vision championed by Bible-inspired missionaries and reformers. These laws stipulated that a Hindu can have only one living spouse at a time. Bigamy, which violates the rights and dignity of the first spouse, would be a crime (unless, of course, the couple first converts to Islam or if the second "partner" accepts the status of being a mistress).

The colonial government had outlawed child marriage in 1929. By then, the case for female education had won popular support. Education requires delaying marriage. Child marriage, however, was more than a legal problem. It was a response to rampant sexual immorality.

---

9. Quoted in "BJP-RSS Has Always Wanted to Change India's Constitution" by Nilanjan Mukhopadyay in *The Wire,* April 20, 2024. see: https://m.thewire.in/article/politics/bjp-rss-has-always-wanted-to-change-indias-constitution/amp (accessed on Dec 25, 2024).

10. B. R. Ambedkar, *Pakistan or the Partition of India,* 1946, pp. 354-355.

Who would ensure that a girl will not be raped and made pregnant? Access to education was limited to urban areas, while most Indians lived in rural areas with limited options for education. The village economy provided few employment opportunities to women. Without either education or employment, what was a girl supposed to do until she was of marriageable age? For reasons such as these, highly respected Hindu leaders such as Bal Gangadhar Tilak (1856–1920) had opposed the ban on child marriage. Marrying daughters before puberty was regarded as a realistic, practical custom.

Intellectual Discrimination

In his classic study, *Modern Religious Movements in India* (1915), J. N. Farquhar highlighted the hopeless state of female education. Before William Carey arrived in Bengal, Farquhar wrote, "Learning had ceased, education was scarce, spiritual religion was only met in quiet places, and women were the saddest victims of this mental and spiritual deprivation."

Carey's own deep grief for India was expressed in his letter to John Williams, the president of his missionary society. He observed, "Women were considered sacrilegious for attempting to develop or use their reasoning powers, as superstitions and moral impurities were not abstract evils but practical consequences that made life hell for the weak."

For a woman, Indian culture was a lethal combination of myths of sexually immoral gods and goddesses. The absence of the Ten Commandments, which required a man to love his own wife, and not his neighbour's, was catastrophic for Indian women. Serving men in complete self-abnegation was a woman's only prospect. Many Hindu temples were dedicated to worshiping goddesses. Some of them had hundreds of temple prostitutes called *devadasis*. These young women were married to gods and taught sexual arts of the *Kama Sutra* to be useful for priests and aristocrats. Some of them also learned dancing. No Hindu sage or ruler championed female education to develop their God-given intellectual potential. It took Christian missionaries such as Hannah Marshman (1767–1847) to take on the challenge of educating Indian women.

Hannah was a huge asset to William Carey's community in Serampore. A warm, pious, and prudent woman, she not only ran her household but also started a boarding school for the children of missionaries and other Europeans. This was an exemplary contrast to what Indian housewives were allowed to do with their lives and talents. At the time of Carey and Marshmann, missionaries did not receive salaries. They had to earn their own living. Hannah's boarding school was a great help in defraying some of the mission's expenses. By the end of the first year 1801, the boarding school showed a profit of Rs. 300. With this success, Mrs. Marshman started schools for Indian boys and girls. Pandits mocked that effort, suggesting that missionaries should try to educate cows. Wiser parents, however, began to enroll their daughters in missionary schools.

The success of that pioneering effort resulted in the establishment of the Calcutta Baptist Female School Society in 1819. During 1820-30, Carey's mission in Serampore took the lead in starting an education revolution for Bengali women, including in rural areas. That led to the founding of girls' schools in Banaras, Dacca, and Allahabad.

The immediate impact of these schools became apparent to many observers. Mrs. Ann Judson, for example, wrote in a letter to her sister about the Mission Charity School near Carey's house: "... with two hundred boys and nearly as many girls—chiefly children picked up from the streets, of no caste. We could see them kneel in prayer together and hear them sing. It was most affecting."

Free schools for low castes and outcastes were always an important feature of the missionary enterprise. The first mission schools were started within a twenty-mile radius of Serampore. Nearly 8,000 children attended these schools. Missionaries did not limit themselves to giving primary education to girls. They launched the Serampore College in order to offer higher education in the vernacular. The Serampore Mission Girls' High School began in 1827. It inspired many initiatives, including Savitri Bai Phule's school for girls, which was founded in 1848 in Pune, Maharashtra. Savitribai Phule along with her husband Jyotirao opened a total of eighteen schools in Maharashtra, teaching children from different castes.

Unfortunately, English-medium schools, started by the East India Company after 1835, began to restrict enrollment mainly to "high" caste students. This discrimination had several reasons:

- High-caste parents did not want their children to sit with low-caste children
- Low-caste parents were unable to pay a school fee
- Many of the teachers hired by the Company brought with them the class prejudices present in English culture
- Some British educators believed that it was enough to educate the higher castes, as wisdom contained in English text books would eventually filter down to lower castes.

British colonial rulers and certain missionaries did not anticipate the possibility that high-caste Hindus might hijack the English language as a tool to discriminate against low-caste Indians. The following incident may better serve to illustrate this point.

Championing Women's Dignity in the South

Nagercoil, mentioned in the beginning of this chapter as the mission field of Charles Mead, was a part of the Hindu kingdom of Travancore. The kingdom was estimated to have had 165,000 to 200,000 slaves. Due to the efforts of missionary campaigns, slaves who worked as bonded tenants in government lands were released in 1836. Missionaries such as Benjamin Bailey, Joseph Peet, and Henry Baker kept pressurising the Travancore kingdom to ban slavery completely. Finally, in 1855, the biblical truth triumphed that "freedom is God's unique gift to humanity made in His image, to serve Him as His children." Slavery was made illegal.

Legalised slavery, however, was only one of the problems. Our culture had invented another tradition to degrade lower-caste women, violate their modesty, and humiliate their men. Force was used to prevent lower-caste women from covering their breasts. Even upper-caste women were required to take off their upper clothing when they went before the priests to worship in a temple or saw a member of the royal family passing by on the street.

In his classic description of Travancore, *The Land of Charity* (1870), Samuel Mateer records an incident in 1828 in which a group of Nadar Christian women went to depose before a lower court. They were forced to remove their upper clothes and leave them at the entrance before entering the Diwan's presence.

Should such a dehumanising culture, which violates a woman's dignity and privacy, be respected? Rev. Mead and other Bible followers could not admire this tradition because they read about a violent man in the New Testament who lived naked in cemeteries. When the Lord Jesus cast out the demon that had possessed him, he sat down at Christ's feet, clothed and in his sound mind. His nakedness was a result of demonic insanity. (Matthew 8:28-34, Mark 5:1-20, and Luke 8:26-39).

The third chapter of the book of Genesis taught Mead that God himself clothed Adam and Eve when nakedness made them too ashamed to come into God's presence. How should missionaries have looked upon our culture that compelled women to remove their upper garment in order to enter a temple? Hindu priests and royalty held sacred their culture, which humiliated others. Bible-believers opposed it as a demonic tradition dishonouring to both God and women.

The clash in perspectives on modesty inspired a revolt against the prohibition of upper clothes. Tranvancore's Hindu queen supported the degradation of women. The campaign to respect women's liberty and defend their modesty was led by Bible-believing missionaries and their wives. They petitioned British officers and Viceroys to use their influence with Hindu kings to respect the dignity of lower caste women.

It took forty years for their efforts to be rewarded, after three revolts in 1822, 1829, and 1855-1859. Ultimately, women from lower castes gained the right to share in equal dignity with upper-caste women. They were permitted to wear an upper garment and cover themselves in public.

Prevailing injustice, inequality, and atrocities against women were not limited to slavery and legal humiliations. As in Bengal, dehumanisation precluded education for women. They were considered unfit to learn even reading and writing. William Tobias Ringeltaube reported, "Girls never come to school in Travancore, which is a great loss." Christian missionaries in the nineteenth century persisted in their efforts to educate women. Mrs. Charles Mead and Mrs. Charles Mault were the first to undertake basic education for women along with teaching the skills of lacemaking and embroidery work. The earnings from lace and embroidery were used to buy their freedom from slavery.

Charles Mead incentivised teachers to bring in slaves to the seminary to learn reading and writing. He offered them cash in return for each slave enrolled. Parents were reluctant to sent their daughters to school because of social norms and poverty. Therefore, missionaries offered free boarding and clothing to the poor students. Only 14 girls joined the first school in 1819. By 1837, the school had 361 girls, and by 1840, 998 girls were enrolled in the mission school. The southern tip of India began to change when boarding schools opened up in places such as Neyyoor, Santhapuram, Parasalai, and Nedumangad. In places where the missionaries could not open boarding schools for girls, they began coeducational schools or Sunday schools to teach reading and writing.

Female missionary educators taught daughters of low-caste families that had converted to Christianity. They also established schools to teach reading and writing to girls from higher castes, because even Brahmins did not educate their women. Brahmin girls shared the same plight of being married in childhood and were often widowed before reaching puberty.

No Hindu sage or ruler highlighted the plight of the high-caste Hindu widow until 1887, when Pandita Ramabai published her book, *The High Caste Hindu Woman*. She was herself a widow, but in defiance of tradition, she had been taught to read and write by her iconoclastic Brahmin father. After becoming a follower of Jesus, Ramabai devoted her life to serving other widows. She knew firsthand the horrible treatment Hindu widows were subjected to. The Bible taught Pandita Ramabai that God's salvation included making us his bride.

Abolishing Sati

An iconic step in reforming India was the abolition of sati—widow burning—in 1829. The practice of sati originated around the fourth century BC within the warrior class in India. Gradually, it grew in popularity as one way to solve the socioeconomic problem that widowhood creates in a joint-family system. Keeping a young widow living in a joint family after the death of her husband makes her an easy prey to the men in the household. What do you do when she gets pregnant?

The Apostle Paul addressed this problem in the New Testament in 1 Timothy 5: he advised younger widows to remarry. That solution of permitting remarriage clashed with the culture of Hindu India: who would pay the dowry (bride price) to the new groom? Who would look after the widow's children from the first husband? Getting rid of the widow appeared to be the simpler solution.

Our sages and priests invented myths to sanctify the horror of murder (or suicide) and soothe the conscience. William Carey, Raja Rammohun Roy, and Tantric scholar Saihardana

Vidyavagish all researched Hindu scriptures to find that the myths justifying sati had little support in ancient religious texts. Polytheism justified sati by promoting the idea that the husband was a wife's god, or "patidev." The Bible opposed the belief that the husband was a wife's god or that a woman's life ceases to be valuable after her husband's death. The Bible's emphasis that God is one—monotheism—implies that everyone must love and serve the true God who created everything and gives value, meaning, and purpose to a woman's life, even after her husband's death.

Cultural practices externalise shared ideas, beliefs, and values. False ideas and myths enslave. They are invented to propagate destructive customs. Therefore, challenging social practices, such as killing newborn girls or burning a widow alive, is a spiritual battle against moral and intellectual darkness.

By the tenth century AD, sati had spread to other southeast Asian countries, including Indonesia, as one solution to the social problem of widowhood. William Carey encountered sati firsthand in 1799. He intervened to prevent it, but the widow insisted on being burnt alive. Every British official in the Company knew of the tradition. Carey opposed it because he believed that "You shall not commit murder" was God's command. Human life is so precious that God incarnated as a human being to give us eternal life. God's word must overrule human culture as well as a widow's "voluntary choice." The choice was not truly voluntary since it was conditioned by man-made myths. Carey's encounter with sati inspired him to conduct careful field research. He turned that research into a powerful paper in 1806. That paper built political support in the campaign against sati.

William Wilberforce, a Member of Parliament, received lists of widows who had committed sati and made it his habit at his dining table to pray against this religious abomination. He distributed Carey's research to fellow MPs to initiate a discussion: Do cultures need to be changed? Should the Bible's worldview serve as the searchlight to help everyone see the dirt that needed to be swept out of British colonies? British intelligentsia knew that the Bible had repeatedly reformed the people of Israel as well as of Europe. The issue was: should its light also reform British colonies?

When the Sanskrit scholar Saihardana Vidyabagish took Raja Ram Mohan Roy to learn English from William Carey, they teamed up to research sati in Sanskrit scriptures. Roy learned that the original and most authoritative Hindu scriptures did not teach sati. The practice originated later. However, sati ceased being an academic issue for Ram Mohan Roy when his own sister-in-law,

Alakamanjari, was forced to die on her husband's funeral pyre He was fond of her and began to realise that far from being "spirituality," the tradition was an abomination based on religious deception and myths. Roy agreed with Carey that Sati needed enlightened governmental intervention as well as a profound change of public opinion at the grassroots. Transforming people's traditions and actions requires changing their beliefs. This was a part of the educational mission. This understanding turned Roy into India's first high-caste social reformer.

Attempts to ban sati had been made earlier. Writing in a monthly magazine in 1751, a Danish missionary described the fate of 47 widows. They had leapt into the flame pit the year before, outside the walls of the Danish colony of Tranquebar.

However intrepid most of those unhappy victims appeared before jumping into the pit, the note was vastly altered when in the midst of the flames: there they shrieked hideously, tumbled one over an-

other, striving to reach the edge of the pit and get out of it, but they were kept in by throwing heaps of billets and faggots upon them, as well to knock them on the head as to increase the fire.

The practice troubled Europe's Christian conscience. The Portuguese banned sati in their territories in Goa as early as 1515. The Dutch and the French followed suit. The Danes allowed it until the nineteenth century. The first formal ban by the British was in 1798, in the city of Calcutta only. Yet, within a 30-mile radius of Calcutta, there were still 300 sati in 1803–1804.

Timid colonial governors, unwilling to interfere with religious customs, shelved the issue until 1829. Approximately 500 to 600 sati occurred every year until the custom was banned in the territories governed by the East India Company. In 1861, Queen Victoria issued a general ban for the whole of India.

The Governor of Bengal issued the edict banning sati in 1829. He asked William Carey to translate it. Carey abandoned his plan to preach that Sunday morning to carry out a "fast unto the Lord" that resulted in widows being legally free to live as human beings. Religion was no longer allowed to orphan a child whose father had died.

The edict was extended to Madras and Bombay in 1830. It took until 1846 for the ban on sati to be adopted by 11 of the 18 independently governed states in India. Finally, the Commission of Sati Prevention Act in 1987 made it illegal throughout India to support, glorify, or commit sati. The punishment was death sentence or life imprisonment for perpetrators. India's culture of murdering widows changed because of the Bible's teaching that God gives life and only He has the right to take it away.

The Root of Female Oppression

The oppression of women is a universal problem. Gender relationships are unequal in most cultures. Women's liberation started in the West because educated career women experienced inequality. They, for example, received less pay than men for the same work. Why are women oppressed?

Indian philosophy, as mentioned earlier, had two explanations for women's subjugation and abandonment: The first was karma and reincarnation. The second was the idea that the male and female binary is an illusion. Everything is One: Brahma. The Bible, on the other hand, explains that a wife's oppression by her husband is a result of the curse upon human sin. One triune God, who is Love, created Adam and Eve to be one in his likeness. Sin damaged their former God-like love, corrupting their relationship into one of subjugation, dominance, and mutual accusation. .

"Sin" is part of the new reality, but hope is found in that the Savior came to save us from sinfulness and restore God's image in us. It is difficult for two sinners to live together "happily ever after." Salvation requires repentance and reconciliation. Reconciliation with God means inviting his Holy Spirit to live in our repentant hearts. God's Spirit produces in his children the fruit of love, joy, forbearance, kindness, goodness, gentleness, and self-control. Such virtues strengthen marriages, women, children, and men.

The Hindu idea of salvation is very different. It is defined as self-realisation, God-realisation, or enlightenment—that is, a perception that I am infinite: God, or Brahman. I am complete. I do not need a wife because male and female energies are already within me.

Biblical marriage is based on the assumption that I, as a man, am finite and a male. Like most males, I need my wife to be whole to be fulfilled as a man. But what if my *Self* is already infinite: Brahman? In that case, my self is already complete. All that is lacking, according to this belief, is that I need to "realise," i.e., experience, my divinity. The journey for self-realisation has to begin with renouncing marriage, abandoning my wife and children, and taking a vow of Brahmacharya and sannyas.

Vedantic/Tantric physiology teaches that every man already has the female energy, or Kundalini Shakti, within him. Normally, it lies dormant, coiled up as a sleeping snake in a psychic center or chakra called Shakti. This chakra is situated at the bottom of the spine, just above the rectum, and is connected to one's sex organs. Self-realisation requires awakening one's female energy, or Kundalini. Usually that requires help from a guru or a partner—male or female. Once awakened, the Kundalini Shakti begins to travel upwards towards the male or Shiva Chakra (psychic center), which is situated on top as the crown. On its way up, the Kundalini passes through five other chakras or psychic centers in one's body. Kundalini's interaction with each of these centers gives different occult/psychic experiences. Finally, when the female Shakti and male Shiva merge in the crown chakra, the meditator experiences his infinite oneness and divinity. That is salvation in Monism or Vedanta (or Oneism). Needless to say, this experience of being one with everything is nothing but a private, subjective feeling. An abandoned wife is all too often the byproduct of this search for self-realisation. Modern law, on the other hand, asserts that the wife abandoned by a mystic in pursuit of his private feelings ought to have the right to divorce him, obtain her share of property, and have the freedom to become one with a husband who will love her.

This fact bears reiterating: a mystical, spiritual Tantric quest begins with rejecting the idea that one is male or female. It requires abandoning one's wife and family in pursuit of one's inner completeness. As was the case of Mahatma Gandhi himself, the religious tradition of Brahmacharya/Sannyas makes a helpless wife a *de facto* widow for the rest of her life.

The Bible's vision of marriage is very different. Brahmacharya or Sannyas require seekers to be single. The Bible's view of marriage begins with God's statement, "It is not good for man to be alone" (Genesis 2:18). Therefore, biblical marriage requires a husband and a wife to be one. As Jesus said, once married, a husband and wife "are no longer two, but one flesh. Therefore, what God has joined together, let no one separate" (Matthew 19:6).

Chapter 6

The Bible and India's Green Revolution[11]

On October 10, 1970, an American agronomist, Norman Borlaugh, was awarded the Nobel Prize for the Green Revolution. He was called "the man who saved a billion lives." India was a land of perennial food shortages and famines. why was it not an Indian who developed a semi-dwarf, high-yield, disease-resistant variety of wheat that could make India a food-exporting nation?

Indians did not lack intelligence by any means. We lacked a worldview that believed that life need not be suffering. We lacked the conviction that hunger and distress could be overcome by human ingenuity because a good God wants to bless his children with abundant life.

Our sages developed abstract philosophies and complex mythologies. Unfortunately, they did not use their minds to tackle the problems of mass hunger and widespread disease. Our educated gurus did nothing for agriculture because it was below the dignity of their caste to work with their hands. They built temples and ashrams on the banks of great rivers as acts of worship but made no effort to build dams and canals to help poor peasants irrigate their farms. Our enlightened yogis and tantric mystics perfected meditation techniques to transcend this world of illusion (maya), but did not develop technologies of food

---

11. I am grateful to Dr. Blesson Paul for his help with this chapter.

production, nor socio-political systems of equitable distribution of food and wealth.

India's Green and White Revolutions were the climax of a Bible-informed intellectual and spiritual movement that began with the Bible translator, William Carey. In the full version of his Nobel Prize Speech, "Lex Prix Nobel en 1970," Norman Borlough summarised the biblical theology of agriculture and abundant life, quoting the following verses from the Bible: Amos 4:9, Joel 1:17,20; Genesis 41:54; Isaiah 8:21; and Isaiah 35:1,7.

My Discovery of India

As mentioned earlier, the city of Allahabad, now called Prayagraj, was my childhood home. As I rode my bicycle to the university as a young man, I often passed in front of Late Pandit Jawaharlal Nehru's home, Anand Bhawan. Nehruji wrote *The Discovery of India,* referred to in Chapter 1. Penned during his imprisonment as a freedom fighter, his book provides a sweeping overview of Indian history, philosophy, and culture. The following summarises my own discovery of my hometown Allahabad, and my country.

Allahabad was founded by the Mughal emperor Akbar, hence a city dedicated to Allah. It was an administrative, military, and cultural center for Islamic rule in India in the 16th and 17th centuries, and continued as such during British colonialism. The city became one of Hinduism's holiest cities, however, because two "holy" rivers, the Ganges and Yamuna, merge there. The Ganges and Yamuna are joined by a third, mythical (invisible) river called the Saraswati. On a daily basis Allahabad attracts hundreds of Hindu worshipers from across India to visit the confluence of these three rivers, the merging of which is called *Sangam.*

Usually pilgrims come to scatter the ashes of their deceased loved ones into the holy waters. During winter, a month-long festival, *Magh Mela,* draws tens of millions to bathe in the Sangam to wash away their sins. The people are drawn by a myth that a drop of the 'Nectar of Life' fell into the Sangam when the gods tricked the demons and flew away with the entire bowl of nectar. The nectar was churned out of the ocean by gods and demons working together. They toiled as a team under an agreement that they would share the fruit of their labour—the Nectar of Life. At the last minute, however, the gods flew away with the nectar, leaving the demons as toiling masses.Once every 12 years, the annual *Magh Mela* festival becomes the *Kumbh Mela,* the largest human gathering in the world. It is claimed that over 660 million pilgrims came to 2025 Kumbh.

Most of these millions of Hindus are from the lower castes, the "common man." The gathering attracts hundreds of thousands of poor beggars, lepers, widows, and orphans. They come seeking alms for temporary relief from hunger, disease, and helplessness.

Every resourceful Hindu—learned philosopher, sage, guru, aristocrat, ruler, or merchant—also comes to bathe in the Sangam at least once in his lifetime. Yet not one of them ever built an institution to change the plight of the poor—our own toiling and starving people.

The mission to change the destiny of local peasants was taken up by an English American philosopher-missionary, Sam Higginbottom. In 1910, he built the Allahabad Agricultural Institute on the banks of the river Yamuna. He sought not only to transform agriculture in north India's fertile plains, but also to change the worldview which had made our toiling masses "backward." The belief system that had distanced our learned men from the plight of the poor masses, was where a fundamental revolution needed to occur.

Higginbottom strove to change India's fatalism and its work ethic which looked down on manual labour. Mahatma Gandhi himself appreciated and embraced the philosophy of working with one's own hands. Gandhi went so far as to require his Brahmin followers, even the Nehru family, to use a spinning wheel and make homespun thread. The thread produced on Indian soil, by Indians, for Indians, was then used then to weave the clothes they would wear. A spinning wheel is still displayed in Nehru's ancestral home, Anand Bhawan, which lies between the university and the Sangam.

Our leaders - men like Gandhi, Nehru, and Pandit Madan Mohan Malviya who wanted to reform India - revered Sam Higginbottom. They saw his Agricultural Institute as a model. On March 15 2000, India's Hindutva Government, led by Prime Minister Atal Bihari Vajpayee, upgraded the institute to the status of a "Deemed University." On 29 December 2016, the Socialist Government of Uttar Pradesh went further. It passed a Legislative Act, making it a full-fledged Christian university, the Sam Higginbottom University of Agriculture, Technology, and Sciences (SHUATS). My older brother, Vinay, studied at the Agricultural Institute in the late 1960s. From 2014-2016, I served there as an honorary professor and the Director of the Center for Human Resource Development.

Life Need Not Be Suffering

Sam Higginbottom, "the Farmer," had studied philosophy at Princeton University in the United States. He came to India to preach salvation to the downtrodden (the Dalits), for Hinduism had taught them they could not be saved unless they were first reincarnated as Brahmins.

Higginbottom's observation of the problem of the poor and his careful study of the Bible inspired him to go back to the USA to study agriculture. He then returned to Allahabad to do what no Indian philosopher, sage, ruler, or businessman had ever done—that is, to make a systematic attempt to fight hunger, eradicate chronic poverty, and modernise agriculture. He rejected Buddhism's First Noble Truth that "Life is suffering" as pessimism. Nor did he accept the Hindu view that life is predetermined to get worse as *Kaliyuga* (the Dark Age) marches down to destruction.

Higginbottom taught the Bible to infuse our culture with hope and perseverance to fight hunger. The poor needed to know God as their Father, who wants to bless his children with abundant life. Poor shepherds needed to know the Good Shepherd, about whom the Psalmist sang, "The Lord is my shepherd/ I lack nothing. He makes me lie down in green pastures/ he leads me beside quiet waters/ he refreshes my soul." (Psalm 23). The revelation was revolutionary: God is not an abstract philosophical theory or a mystical experience, but our Father, who wants to be our shepherd, if we choose to be his sheep.

Higginbottom persuaded the education establishment to grant academic respectability to the study of agriculture, horticulture, dairy farming, and related subjects such as agro-engineering and food processing. The shudras (untouchables)—blacksmiths and carpenters—who strive to make better tools for agriculture ought to be commended as innovative engineers.

Sam Higginbottom penned the worldview that inspired his mission in a book, *The Gospel and the Plow*. He taught the gospel so that we Indians would seek God's kingdom here on this earth. The Green Revolution succeeded because missionaries like him had begun to produce the manpower that could benefit from the advanced research of scientists such as Norman Borlaugh. Higginbottom, who inspired Indian leaders, including Madan Mohan Malviya, Motilal, Jawaharlal Nehru and Mahatma Gandhi, was well aware that he was just one of the runners in a long relay race that the Bible had started through Charles Grant (1746-1823). Many other missionaries, civil servants, magistrates, military leaders, and engineers had been engaged in changing India's culture of indifference and hopeless resignation.

Charles Grant, Agriculture, and Nationalism

Grant arrived in India in 1767, a mere two years after the Mughal Emperor met with the East India Company at Allahabad Fort. The Allahabad Fort had been commissioned in 1583 by Emperor Akbar; it was the largest fort he built, a symbol of Muslim power and prestige in the subcontinent. Akbar's weaker descendant Emperor Shah Alam II handed over to the Company the authority to administer "Bengal," including Bangladesh, in 1765. No one had trained the Company's young Englishmen the art and ethics of governing.

Two years after arriving in Bengal, Grant witnessed firsthand the disastrous famine of 1769–73. It devastated over 20 million powerless people and accounted for a death toll between 7 - 10 million.

Grant learned that famines were a regular feature of the Indian subcontinent, which depended on monsoon rains for irrigation. No Hindu, Buddhist, or Muslim ruler had ever taken serious steps to change that natural reality of frequent famines by conserving water in dams or reservoirs for agriculture. Rulers did not even build warehouses to store grain as a precaution against years of drought. Three primary reasons accounted for the lack of food storage. Firstly, prior to the agricultural revolution, farming did not yield significant surpluses. Secondly, unjust taxation laws robbed peasants of the motivation to produce a surplus even if the land yielded it. Lastly, centuries of rule by a succession of kings, conquerors, and emperors had failed to build a significant infrastructure of roads, bridges, or tunnels to transport grain from one part of India to another. The transportation of high-value products, such as grain, needed security and insurance.

The famine that Grant and others witnessed and described had a lasting impact on the Indian psyche. A century later, in 1882, another British civil servant, Bankim Chandra Chatterjee, penned his classic novel *Anand Math*. His story of Hindu-Muslim conflict is set against the backdrop of that famine. This same novel also popularised Chatterjee's song *Bande Mataram*, which became a strong contender to become India's national anthem.

Indian publishers routinely omit the novel's last chapter, which is included in various editions, such as the one published by the Oxford University Press. That concluding chapter says that after defeating the Muslims, the victors, the Hindu *Sannyasins* (ascetics), decide next to wage war against British Colonialism. Their heavenly guide stops them, explaining to them the Biblical concept of Providence. God who governs history, the guide says, has sent the British to India to teach us practical matters of science and technology, agriculture and business, law and commerce, management, and leadership. Once we have learned these useful subjects, God himself will take the British rulers back to England.

Bankim Chandra, one of our first nationalist novelists, knew how Charles Grant and others had responded to the awful sufferings inflicted by famine. The horror of that tragedy made Grant a prophet of modern education and agriculture for India. He believed the Bible's teaching that human suffering was contrary to God's will. The Creator had intended human beings to live in a garden—in abundance. Sin had driven man out of the garden, to the jungles and slums. Sin is rebellion against God. It makes us enemies of our loving Father. It makes us Satan's slaves. God sent the Savior, Jesus Christ, to save us from our sin and therefore from Satan's kingdom and the slums.

The Lord Jesus came to give us abundant life. That was also the purpose of God's invitation to Abraham to leave his homeland and culture to walk in friendship with God. If he did, God would give his offspring a land flowing with milk and honey. They would become a blessing and a light of hope to the nations.

Grant learned that the Bible was not a fatalistic but an optimistic book. It began to be written when God delivered Abraham's descendants from Egypt's slavery in order to fulfill his promise of *shalom*—the peace that comes from freedom from tyranny, justice under the rule of law, and brings economic progress through diligent work, private ownership, and the security of wealth.

In 1792, Charles Grant followed the suggestion of an Evangelical Member of Parliament, William Wilberforce, to write down his *Observations* of life in South Asia and his prescription for changing the land that the Company was governing. The Company needed to improve Indian agriculture and economy. At first Grant's book was hand-copied for the Members of Parliament who were called to renew the East India Company's Charter in 1793. The book was printed in 1797. In 1812, the British Parliament published it as a State Paper which made a lasting influence upon the civil servants who governed India.

Grant advocated that Britain should cultivate the use of reason among Indians by teaching English to improve vernacular. Missionaries should be sent to teach natural sciences and mechanical arts to steward nature (rather than merely escape it) to reduce toil and increase productivity through inventions. Further, taxation must be fair to incentivise wealth creation.

Grant's younger contemporary, William Carey who established the first mission in Bengal, began implementing Grant's prophetic vision for transforming Indian agriculture and economy.

William Carey and the Agri-Horticultural Society

The linguistic work of this humble British cobbler turned Bible translator produced novelists such as Bankim Chandra Chatterjee and poets such as Nobel Laureate Rabindranath Tagore. They used Carey's Bengali as they injected the Bible's world-changing worldview and nationalism into Bengal.

Carey's marble bust will greet you if you visit the Agri-Horticultural Society of India in Kolkata. No such society existed anywhere in the world when Carey founded it in 1820. If you ask the Society's receptionists, they will show you the Minutes of the Society's early meetings, all written in Carey's handwriting. Reading those Minutes will help you understand what missionaries did to bring new crops, fruits, and flowers into India, as well as how they built models and innovative programs, fairs, competitions, and incentives to improve production and methods of agriculture and horticulture.

Carey, the linguist, translator, and mentor to civil servants, pioneered systematic research into agriculture in Bengal. Before him, no Hindu or Muslim saint or scholar had done anything comparable. He published his findings in the *Journal of Asiatic Society*.

Carey made pioneering contributions to the study and teaching of botany. Many Hindu ashrams were built on the banks of perennial rivers, yet not one of them developed a botanical garden. This was not because Brahmins lacked the ability. The problem was that our mythologies and philosophies did not teach that Adam and Eve were created to cultivate and steward a garden. There was no divine mandate to study nature in order to establish human dominion over it. Knowledgeable sages who did find therapeutic herbs, leaves, fruit, and roots did not establish medical colleges to transmit their medical expertise. They knew that knowledge was power. Thus, they kept it strictly within the family, passing on their secret remedies only to their sons.

Carey learned and introduced the Linnaean system of gardening developed by Carl Linneaus, the son of a Lutheran pastor and gardener in Sweden. Linnaeus learnt more from his father than Latin names for plants. He also received the Bible's view of creation: "The observer of nature sees, with admiration, that the whole world is full of the glory of God." This was the opposite of the Hindu view of the physical world as Maya—illusory deception. Carey's botanical garden in Serampore became India's second-best after Kolkata's. His dedication to science, the environment, and botany led to the naming of the 'Careya' genus in his honour.

The Bible's teaching that God had declared the material world to be good encouraged William Carey to study plants and teach botany and forestry. This was an aspect of the biblical mission because the Creator had commissioned human beings to manage the earth on their Father's behalf. Human sin brought a curse upon the land that it would grow thorns and thistles and man will have to toil: eat of the sweat of his brow. The good news (the Gospel) is that our sin and the curse it incurred were nailed to Christ's cross on Calvary. Through him, we can find forgiveness and reconciliation with our Father. The earth, groaning under the curse, eagerly waits for the mutual deliverance of the children of God and nature (Romans 8:20–24). The Bible's promise of the earth's renewal inspired William Carey to advocate for the cultivation of wastelands and the teaching of forestry. His advocacy of the light revealed in the Bible about nature, its problems, and renewal became the catalyst for later government initiatives in several spheres. Such initiatives challenged the prevailing pessimistic resignation and brought India out of the middle ages.

Harnessing, Not Worshipping, the Ganges River

Many officers of the British army were trained at the Addiscombe Military Academy. They studied subjects such as drafting, surveying, fortifications, mathematics, classics, and Indian languages. The brightest students were reserved for the Engineer Corps.

Around 1818-19, a young cadet named Proby Thomas Cautley attended the academy. Like many others, he was the son of a godly pastor. Cautley and nine of his fellow students joined the engineering corps, where many of them played pivotal roles in designing public works such as dams, canals, and railways. They had little time to engage in military matters.

Cautley became the superintendent of the Ganges Canal projects. Learned gurus worshipped the holy river Ganges and meditated on its banks, seeking salvation. They also invented rituals such as *Varuna Yajna* or *Parjanya Yajna* to appease the god of rain, Varuna. One such ritual, still practiced in distressed times, required dozens of naked women to plough the fields while the priests recited sacred mantras.[12]

Cautley surveyed the river to contemplate harnessing its waters to save north India from cyclical hunger and famines. He faced complex challenges with limited resources. One challenge was that capable Hindu entrepreneurs had built many temples and ashrams on the banks of sacred rivers. Christian engineers and administrators had to appease devotees by offering to build bathing ghats that could be used safely even during the monsoon season when the rivers were flooded. The British Parliament paid for the construction of the Ganga Barrage and Canal to irrigate "Doab," the land between two rivers, Ganga and Yamuna. The project required more engineers, however. Cautley proposed to establish a civil engineering college so that bright Indians could learn to rule over rivers instead of worshipping them.

James Thomason, the Lieutenant Governor of the North-Western Provinces, actively supported Cautley's idea and helped establish India's first engineering college. It began in Roorkee in 1848 as the Thomason College of Engineering. A century later, the Pandit Nehru-led government of independent India elevated it to become India's first engineering university. In 2001, the Vajpayee-led Hindu government of India renamed it the Indian Institute of Technology (IIT), Roorkee.

The opening of the Ganges canals in April 1854 was a historic event which transformed more than irrigation and agriculture. It injected into the Indian soul the Bible's idea that human beings ought to worship their Creator and establish their dominion over the creation. Hundreds of thousands of people attended the inaugural ceremony, including the Maharaja of Gwalior. Two generations later, one of his descendants became a financial supporter of Sam Higginbottom and the Allahabad Agriculture Institute.

British engineers and their Indian pupils completed the Lower Ganges Canal system between 1872 and 1878. That resulted in the construction of more than a thousand miles of main channels,

---

12. https://www.deccanherald.com/specials/bizarre-indian-practices-to-attractrain-739743.html

irrigating over 1.5 million acres in the most densely inhabited part of India.

Developing India's human potential has been even more crucial than building canals. A number of Roorkee IIT alumni have gone on to play significant roles in India's technological development. They have received prestigious awards and occupy prominent positions in the government and private sectors of the industry.

Godavari Dam

The vision for the Ganges Canal system was inspired by what had already been done for the Godavari river delta. The Godavari is one of south India's mightiest rivers as it crosses from west to east. Frequent floods in its delta region in southeast India created havoc and precluded the possibility of building a strong industrial and economic culture. Sir Arthur Cotton (1803-1899), a British engineer, faced intense criticism, stiff opposition, and even impeachment proceedings, but he persevered to build the Godavari Barrage and canal system. His determination transformed the area into the "Rice Bowl of India."

Sir Arthur Cotton came from a family of evangelists. At the age of 18, he joined the British East India Company's military engineering corps. His dedication enabled him to ascend the ranks quickly to become a captain. In 1832–33, a devastating famine struck the coastal districts of Rajahmundry, resulting in widespread suffering and loss of life. Captain Cotton was assigned the task of assessing the situation. His report identified poor irrigation practices as a root cause of the famine. He urged British superiors in government to intervene.

But why should Britain intervene, when no Indian ruler had addressed the issue before? Wasn't life suffering? Wasn't suffering a consequence of karma? Could the future be better than the present?

The British sought to build a network of railways which would increase their revenue from Indian goods, and make it possible to move their armies quickly when needed. Cotton argued passionately that investing in irrigation infrastructure to increase agricultural production would uplift the poor and generate even greater productivity, and therefore revenue. He had already built a barrage for the Kollidam River in

Tamil Nadu, a success which supported his case. Yet the technical challenge of damming the Godavari was staggering. The river's discharge was immense over a vast basin. But Cotton persisted, undergirded by his belief in a Creator God who had called people to establish dominion over the earth. Canal irrigation would reduce farmers' dependence on unpredictable monsoons and boost food production. Regulating river waters would also make it possible to build secure housing and industries.The Godavari Barrage was completed in 1852. In 1970, the Indian government renamed it Sir Arthur Cotton Barrage. To this day, it provides irrigation for about 364,000 acres of fertile agricultural land.

Redefining the Path of Knowledge

The Path of Knowledge, or *Jnana Marga,* is one of Hinduism's most important paths of salvation. The sages that followed this path of "knowledge" were second to none in intelligence or dedication. Yet none of them studied or taught agriculture to pave the way for India's Green Revolution. The revolution that transformed India into a food-exporting country was the work of the Nobel Prize-winning American scientist Norman Bourlaug, "the man who saved a billion lives."

Bourlaug was born in a Lutheran family on a farm in Iowa in 1914. His adolescence and young adulthood in the United States were marked by the Great Depression of 1929-1939. The horrors of his times could have pushed him into an escapist spirituality. His Lutheran environment and farming background, however, encouraged him to become an agricultural scientist. The wife of German reformer Martin Luther, Katherine von Bora, had injected the"Protestant work ethic" into Lutheran spirituality of 16th century Europe The Protestant work ethic was transplanted to the New World at the founding of Puritan North American colonies, a worldview I have discussed in greater detail in *This Book Changed Everything*. After earning a Ph.D. in Plant Pathology, Borlaug went to Mexico in 1944 to serve farmers there. Due to a dreaded stem rust disease, these farmers were producing only half the wheat their fields were capable of. For thirteen long years, Borlaug and his team researched ways to develop enhanced wheat breeds that eventually increased Mexico's crop sixfold.

In the 1950s and 1960s, India was struggling with its own food shortages. The US government was providing aid, but India possessed untapped capacity to produce enough food for itself and others. Through channels such as the Rockefeller and Ford foundations, the US government offered scientific knowledge to improve India's agriculture. The India Agriculture Program (IAP) was launched.

In 1965, Prime Minister Indira Gandhi and Dr. M.S. Swaminathan sought Norman Borlaug's help. Borlaug trained Indian scientists to produce high-yielding semi-dwarf wheat seeds that were resistant to stem rust and other diseases. Their efforts met obstacles in implementation, however, because of the Indian government's socialist policies and bureaucratic delays. Against the advice of officials, Borlaug confronted a disease even more devastating than the fungus of wheat stem rust: the socialism that Mrs. Gandhi's father, Pandit Jawaharlal Nehru, had imported from Russia and European academia.

Eventually, Borlaug's scientific guidance and Bible-based philosophy of economic liberty paved the way for India's Green Revolution. That philosophy relied upon the citizen's freedom from the government and its ideologically driven bureaucratic experts. Individual liberty requires personal development, initiative, responsibility, and inner discipline.

The Green Revolution succeeded because Mrs. Gandhi was willing to listen to wise counsel and change some of her government's policies. Today, India produces ample food. The agricultural sector is the largest source of livelihood in India, and the country is one of the world's largest food producers and exporters. Turning its back on progress, the Hindutva movement governing India now condemns the biblical spirituality which had blessed the country with abundance. Hindutva invests far more energy and resources to instigate hatred against the Bible than in encouraging research and innovation to build India into a greater nation.

Chapter 7

The Bible, Not Britain, Modernised India

My wife Ruth and I both grew up in urban Uttar Pradesh. In January 1976, six months after our marriage, we moved to a village outside of Chhatarpur in Madhya Pradesh to live and work with the rural poor. We began to hear stories that made no sense: "A young man was beaten up today because he rode a new bicycle into the village." The next day, "Another young man was stripped and beaten because he wore a new terylene shirt."

Why? What was going on?

It did not take long for us to learn that our feudal-era village culture was going through historic social changes. The landless poor—the low castes—had started going to Punjab during the harvest season. Manual harvesting is backbreaking labour. Mechanical harvesters had not reached most of Punjab. After harvesting Punjabi fields manually, those poor families returned to rural Madhya Pradesh with bags of food and some cash. Some of them bought a few good clothes. A few even had the audacity to buy "luxury" items such as bicycles! Bicycles were liberating. Low caste men who owned a bicycle did not have to work for the village landlords. They could pedal to the city and work for cash as casual labourers. Such economic liberty infuriated high caste landlords.

Until then, the low-caste, landless labourers were tasked with looking after the cattle of high caste Hindus or tilling their fields. In return, they were mostly given food, not cash. Now, the opportunities in Punjab and the bicycles were making it hard for high castes to get labourers. The display of wealth, i.e., better clothes and bicycles, irritated the low-minded "high" castes. After all, it had been self-evident to them, their sages and scriptures, that the gods and karma had permanently denied women and "low" castes inalienable rights to liberty or the "pursuit of happiness."

A more disruptive factor was the Land Ceiling Act No. 13 of 1974. It built upon the Land Reform movement, which had begun two centuries earlier and gathered momentum after Independence in 1947. The Act limited how much agricultural land an individual or family could own. Any surplus land was confiscated from the landlords and given to the landless. For generations, landless labourers had cultivated the farms owned by the higher castes. Now they were being given the ownership of those lands. This was a revolution. In theory, it meant that the poor could now work their fields for themselves, their children, and their grandchildren.

Owning land meant acquiring equity. The poor could now borrow loans against this property to dig wells, educate their children, or build better homes. An unforeseen problem was created now: who would cultivate the lands that high caste landlords owned? Working with their own hands was beneath the dignity of their caste. Land reform was robbing the landlords of the privileges that caste, karma, gods, and Hindu scriptures had bestowed upon them.

Freedom: Economic and Religious

This socio-economic revolution was called "*Sarvodaya*": Upliftment of All. Its seed was sown into Mahatma Gandhi's soul by John Ruskin's 1860 book, *Unto This Last*. In 1904, Mahatma Gandhi read the book during a train ride in South Africa. It impacted him so deeply that in 1908, he paraphrased and published it in Gujarati as *Sarvodaya*.

The book is Ruskin's exposition of one of Christ's parables about the Kingdom of God. The Bible records it in the Gospel of Matthew 20:1-16. Jesus' parable implies that Satan's kingdom oppresses and exploits the weak. God's kingdom liberates and empowers the marginalised people whom the prophet Isaiah called "a bruised reed, a flickering flame."

After Gandhi returned to India, he attempted to infuse this aspect of Christ's perspective on spirituality into the Indian National Congress. This was a historic challenge to the hierarchical Indian culture that denied human equality on principle. Inspired by the Bible, Mahatma Gandhi sought to change an elitist Congress into a mass movement of freedom and upliftment for all.

The biblical value of sarvodaya, or the upliftment of all perceived religious or caste-based land ownership as an important root of poverty. Therefore, it sought to transform ownership in rural India. That, however, was a threat to established religion and social order. This was not socialism. The Bible's secondbook, called Exodus, records the history of Israel's freedom from Egyptian slavery. The newborn nation of Israel was brought to inherit its own "promised land." Political freedom on its own has little value without economic freedom or property rights. The prophet Ezekiel summarised this biblical idea of land rights when he wrote:

"The prince must not take any of the inheritance of the people, driving them out of their property. He is to give his sons their inheritance out of his own property so that not one of my people will be separated from their property." (Ezekiel 46: 18)

Prior to independence, in the first half of the 1900s, only a few Indians were wealthy. The middle class, which is now about 30% of the population, hardly existed. Three out of four people survived on subsistence agriculture. Famines were frequent, and millions died because of malnutrition and disease. Most peasants had neither jobs nor land. They had no access to higher education, good healthcare, or affordable credit. Power, transportation, and legal infrastructure were necessary to produce and market goods and services. Train service between Bombay and Thane began in 1853 under the British Raj. Public bus service started only in 1926 in Bombay. Gandhi's protégé Pandit Jawaharlal Nehru, had the responsibility of tackling these challenges after he became India's Prime Minister. Prior to that, in *The Discovery of India* Nehru observed that,

"There was a lack of food, of clothing, of housing, and of every other essential requirement of human existence... The development policy objective should be to get rid of the appalling poverty of the people."

Freedom: Political and Cultural

Indians did not elect British rulers. For that matter, India never elected Muslim, Sikh, Buddhist, or Hindu rulers either. None of our pre-modern rulers, therefore, had any reason to develop agriculture to produce food for the hungry. Rulers pay attention to the citizens if the people who elect them can replace them.

Pandit Nehru and Dr. Ambedkar knew how Moses transformed wandering Israelite slaves into a great nation. Unlike Mughal emperors, Moses did not appoint nawabs to rule over the people. If he did, the nawabs would be loyal to Moses, not to the people. Moses asked the people to choose their own elders from their own tribes. These elected leaders would be men they knew and trusted for their wisdom and integrity (Deuteronomy 1:13). The elders, Moses knew, would need God's Spirit to govern a people as difficult as the Israelites (Deut 1:12–17). Nevertheless, it was important for governing elders to be accountable to the people they were chosen to serve.

The Apostle John's vision of heaven in Revelation 4:4 is a picture of the Bible's philosophy of governance. Elders sit on thrones around God's central throne. They wear golden crowns on their heads because they manage God's kingdom, ensuring that God's will is done on earth. Such a philosophy of governance was very different from the brutal empires of the Romans or the Mughals.

John's readers knew Rome's beastly empire. Wicked gangsters such as Herod who took his brother's wife, killed newborn boys around Bethlehem and beheaded John the Baptist, bribed Roman emperors to acquire the right to rule little kingdoms. Such beastly rulers obtained the right to extract taxes and bribes from the people. That is slavery or colonialism. Freedom, in contrast, gives political power, sovereignty and rights to citizens.

John's vision in Revelation 4 was an exposition of Daniel's vision of

God's humane kingdom. Six centuries before Christ, the prophet Daniel foresaw that the Messiah's coming would change global governance. In his vision, Daniel recorded the brutality of the beastly kingdom: "But the court will sit and his [the beast's] power will be taken away and completely destroyed forever. Then the sovereignty, power, and greatness of all the kingdoms under heaven will be handed over to the holy people of the Most High." (Daniel 7: 26-27)

The Constitution of India expressed this concept of the people's sovereignty in its opening phrase, "We, the people of India..." School children are taught that the Constituent Assembly copied those words from the United States Constitution. That is correct. But our Constitution was not a cut-and-paste job. We borrowed such phrases because our leaders and the Constituent Assembly understood and agreed with the ideas expressed in those words. What our teachers don't tell us, and many do not even know, is that the concept of popular sovereignty came to the USA and into India from the Bible.

It is common knowledge that in his Gettysburg Address of 1863, President Abraham Lincoln defined democracy as "Government of the people, for the people, and by the people." What most people never hear is that President Lincoln was quoting John Wycliffe (1330-1384). Wycliffe was an eminent theology professor at Oxford University who elevated the Bible to a place of supremacy for the church, insisting that the Bible should be made available to all Christians in their own language. He was the first to translate the Bible from the Latin Vulgate into old English. Wycliffe captured part of the Bible's political essence in the preface to his translation. He wrote, "This book is for [the] government of [the] people, by [the] people, and for [the] people."

Pandit Nehru needed Indians to vote for him. Why then was he offending the high caste landlords by taking away their lands and giving them to the poor? He knew Christ's teaching in the Beatitudes

"Blessed are you who are poor,
for yours is the kingdom of God.
Blessed are you who hunger now,
for you will be satisfied.

Blessed are you who weep now,
for you will laugh." (Luke 6: 20-21)

Implications For Property Rights

Colonial rulers did not represent the people. Unlike Nehru, much of their early interest in agriculture was focused on exporting opium to east and southeast Asia, particularly China. The East India Company assigned itself an exclusive monopoly for this profitable trade.

Elitist neglect of agriculture was only one of India's economic problems. Equally important was Europe's Industrial Revolution. Europe's industrialisation was strangling India's pre-modern cottage industry. Should colonial rulers empower Indians to counter the European Industrial Revolution by industrialising India? No Hindu or Muslim ruler was attempting that in the state he ruled.

Inspired by John Ruskin's opposition to the Industrial Revolution, Mahatma Gandhi attempted to save the traditional cottage industry. His solution was the spinning wheel! He burned factory-made clothes and wore handmade *khadi*, fabric woven with hand-spun thread. Nehru, however, replaced Gandhi's naivete with realism: tractors destroy ox-carts and computers kill the typewriter industry. Therefore, the challenge of the Industrial Revolution had to be met head-on by industrialising India. We needed cotton mills, not spinning wheels in every home.

Transforming a rural/agricultural society into an industrial nation required education, banking, power generation, transportation, and communication. It was equally important to build a just legal and political system that was responsive and accountable to the people. No government, before British colonial rule, had ever invested in India's future because none had been elected by the people. Muslims, for example, ruled Delhi for well over seven centuries, from 1192 to 1858. They built great monuments and forts but not one college, university, or even a hospital.

The British defeated the Mughal empire by military prowess. Power breeds arrogance. It is sustained by keeping subjects ignorant and weak. That is why many English rulers opposed the evangelical advocacy for educating Indians. For thousands of years, Brahminism had retained its power by keeping women and Shudras "backward": uneducated, unarmed, and poor. Dr. Bhimrao Ambedkar emphasised the need to educate the downtrodden in order to uplift India. Ambedkar publicly burned the *Manusmriti* in 1927 with the bold claim that making India a Hindu nation, governed by Hindu scriptures, would be the greatest imaginable calamity, because the sovereignty of mentally enslaved people has little meaning.

However, colonial rulers, like Brahmins, Mughals, or Marathas, had no reason to empower Indians. Uplifting India intellectually, economically, physically, and politically had to be a mission driven by love and an understanding of God's will for humanity. Transforming traditional hierarchical culture required self-sacrificing, cross-bearing visionaries. That was exactly what the Bible had inspired Europe's reformers to do. The nineteenth-century missionary movement brought to India that intellectual revolution based on the knowledge of God. European states that supported godly, biblical, moral church-sponsored education prospered. Those that suppressed it have remained weaker until today.

Why did Nehru take land from the landlords and give it to their former slaves—the landless Shudras? Was it because he understood or followed the Bible? That is a question for others to study in depth and document.

Today, many Hindutva leaders praise the militant Hindu Nathuram Godse, for assassinating Mahatma Gandhi during a multi-faith prayer meeting. Most of them also attack Nehru as anti-Hindu. That, however, does not imply that all of Nehru's economic policies were derived from the Bible. He attempted to liberate low caste landless labourers from bondage to high caste feudal landlords in order to make everyone's creative energy available for national development. At the same time, however, his socialism enslaved the people to a state-owned, corrupt, and inefficient industrial-bureaucratic establishment. The Bible has yet to liberate India from Nehru's socialism as well as from Modi's "Hindu capitalism." That is a subject for another chapter.

Colonialism's Balance Sheet

The British East India Company governed much of South Asia until the great Revolt of 1857. Following that, the British Crown disbanded the Company and took over governance. Indians call that revolt the 'First War of Independence', even though the rebels made an incompetent descendent of the Mughals as India's ruler in place of the East India Company. The British labeled the revolt a "mutiny" because it began with Indian soldiers serving the British Company. Quickly, however, the rebellion spread beyond the army. Civilian uprisings arose and threatened the Company rule. Eventually the British Crown stepped in and reorganised governance, the army, the financial system, and India's administration.

The British rule, like other governments, impacted India both for good as well as for evil. Some day a macro-historian will prepare a credible balance sheet without current biases and vested interests. The beneficial impacts included giving India the idea of a nation, education, a legal system that respected human rights and individual liberty, a clean administration and judiciary, and a professional military.

An honest academic study of the Bible's impact on colonial governance and India's social reform will take serious and sustained funding. Scholars will need to study the Bible's impact on the Magna Carta, the development of British Law and freedom, and the English Civil War, which established the principle that the law was above the king (*Lex Rex*). A biblical theology of Law is necessary in order to grasp why the British Parliament tried Robert Clive in 1772 and Warren Hastings in 1788 on corruption charges. Those two men had won India for Britain.

From 1947 well into the 1960s, India's central and state governments continued the colonial tradition of corruption-free governance. Now, in the absence of the Bible's moral underpinning, it has become practically impossible for the Indian Parliament to investigate corruption charges against the ruling party or its financiers. An earlier chapter has already discussed how the Bible reformed British rule in India. This current chapter is primarily about the Bible's role in liberating India from the culture that had stifled its progress.

Today, India is strong. In the 1750s and 60s, a tiny trading company was able to colonise the vast Mughal Empire. That raises the question: why couldn't Hindus liberate themselves from Muslim and Sikh rules? Did our culture make us weak and vulnerable? What revived and empowered us? British rule or the missionary movement?

This chapter is not about the missionary movement. My other books, such as *The Father of Modern India: William Carey*; *Missionary Conspiracy: Letters to a Postmodern Hindu*, and *India: The Grand Experiment* have discussed the role that Christian missions played in creating modern India. India Research 75 is preparing a multi-volume study to investigate missionary movement's cultural impact. This chapter can look only at some aspects of the Bible that India chose to follow in order to govern itself.

A Company which existed to generate wealth for its owners had no reason to transform India into a dynamically developing nation. That's why it was the Bible, not colonialism, that transformed our culture and character.

Culture: From Caste Discrimination to Property Rights

The revenue that the East India Company generated through trade is documented in its records. It benefited the Company's owners, not the staff. Once they acquired the power to govern, the Company's servants were able to rob their subjects. The bribes that the Company's staff extorted were not recorded in any official ledgers. Christian statesmen objected to this robbery because the Bible forbids theft and unjust gain. It also taught that God wanted to bless all nations, including India, and make it a great nation. Britain's Christian statesmen reasoned that God's command, "Love your neighbour as yourself," meant giving to India as good a government as British citizens wanted for themselves. Christ's Golden Rule: "Do to others as you would have them do unto you" (Luke 6:31), must be followed.

The Company's corruption was a new problem. The corruption of an entrenched caste system had already weakened the masses for thousands of years prior to the arrival of Europeans. The Indian name for caste is *Varnashram Dharma*. It prevented women and lower castes from developing their potential to create and enjoy wealth. Not allowing Shudras to read Sanskrit Scriptures or enter Hindu temples was religious discrimination. Their economic deprivation, including landlessness, was a part of an ancient culture that perpetually excluded them from gaining the power of knowledge, arms, property, or productivity.

The Dalit farm labourers who returned from Punjab to their villages in Madhya Pradesh with their modest earnings were beaten in order to remind them of their social standing. Hindu culture had reserved economic, political, and social power solely for the higher castes. In the democratic India of the 1980s, persecution of the lower castes actually became the impetus for mobilising them into a political force, the Bahujan Samaj Party (BSP). Moreover, low castes that had been oppressed as Hindus for centuries were motivated by the Ambedkar movement to convert out of Hinduism to other religions. Public attention was drawn to the fact that an entrenched worldview, not Europeans, had robbed the lower castes of financial freedom and weakened India as a nation.

The Biblical Background of Nehruvian Land Reforms

Independent India's government under Nehru did not invent land reforms. It continued the transformation that the Bible had inspired almost two centuries earlier. Statesmen such as Edmund Burke, Charles Grant, Henry Dundas, William Wilberforce, William Pitt, and others had already used political power to begin to change India's unjust socioeconomic system. Grant's first-hand experience in Bengal helped him realise that land reforms were among India's fundamental needs. Land ownership, secure property rights, a fair, equitable, and affordable justice system, and an educated cadre of patriots were essential for lifting India out of its poverty.

British statesmen learned, as did the initial Indian governments, that political power can corrupt culture more easily than improve it. Politics flows downstream from culture. Culture is created by a people's beliefs, ideas, ideals, and values—in short, their worldview. Changing a worldview is one of the purposes of education. That is why Charles Grant became "the prophet of India's education."

The book of Exodus, the second book of the Bible, describes the steps God took to transform Hebrew slaves into a wise, great, and prosperous nation. One factor was to cultivate deep religious respect for other people's property rights. The Israelites were liberated from Egypt's slavery so that each family may own its own land and enjoy the fruit of their own labours. This motif of private property (or the right to pursue happiness) was summed up in the vision that in the Promised Land, "They shall sit every man under his vine and under his fig tree, and no one shall make them afraid" (Micah 4:4). That vision of private property and economic liberty became one of the most important motifs that compelled George Washington's fight against British imperialism.

Education transforms a nation into a great one if it includes ethical character training. Schools and colleges need to do more than merely impart information to students and develop their skills. To educate is to cultivate the fear of God, which is the beginning of wisdom (Proverbs 9:1). Until the 1830s in Europe, education was the Church's ministry of "disciplining nations." It taught Christian statesmen the secrets of the economic success of Protestant Europe. One of those secrets was that every child memorised the Ten Commandments recorded in Exodus 20. The tenth commandment, "You shall not covet" what belongs to another, means you shall create for yourself the wealth that you desire.

Likewise, God's command against stealing implied that colonial civil servants needed to learn that extracting bribes was disobedience to God. Indians also needed to learn God's commandments. Why would a peasant grow mangos, papayas, or tomatoes if upper caste bullies could just take such produce from him without reimbursing him? Why would an innovator spend time, energy, and resources to develop a gadget or an intellectual property if his society does not ensure that he would earn a living from his intellectual property?

Indians did not lack the ability to grow food or innovate ideas and products. We lacked the Ten Commandments and, therefore, a culture conducive to creativity. In 1976, when Ruth and I started our rural development service in Chhatarpur (MP), we were amazed to discover that 75% of our vegetables were coming from Nashik, 1,140 kilometers away! Horticulture alone could have eradicated poverty. But to grow good mangoes was to invite trouble—bullies, not traders!

Cultivating the mind and developing skills—i.e., education—takes years of hard work. Creating a culture that respects a neighbor's produce, property and family requires transforming religion. Innovation involves risk-taking and failures. Such investments are worthwhile only if one's culture is ethical and if others don't pirate your produce or intellectual properties. An ethical culture which promotes creative risk-taking and productivity simultaneously must prohibit coveting and stealing. The state can pass laws, but it cannot build that kind of ethical culture. The fear of God is inculcated as a matter of the heart. That is the role that education and the church play. That's why William Wilberforce and others in the English evangelical movement asked Parliament to permit missionaries to go to India and educate its young men.

Six decades ago, when I was a teenager, when a person referred to someone as "an educated man," he meant a civilised, trustworthy gentleman. That is no longer the case. Now being an "educated person" simply means having a degree with a layer of external polish, not someone who has cultivated the virtues of inner integrity or trustworthiness.

The Beginning of Land Reforms

India has a history and prehistory that goes back at least four thousand years. During these millennia, many civilisations arose and fell. None of them, however, gave India a legal system conducive to socio-economic development. In *Truth and Transformation: A Manifesto for Ailing Nations,* I have discussed the economic implications of each of the Ten Commandments.

Pitt's India Act of 1784 was one of the first attempts to rationalise how the Company ought to govern Bengal. William Pitt the Younger was a close friend of William Wilberforce, the evangelical Member of Parliament whose contributions to modern India we have already discussed. Pitt was the abolitionist Prime Minister who banned British companies from buying and selling African slaves. Pitt's Act of 1784 began to institutionalise property rights, particularly through the reforms of Lord Cornwallis. Gandhi's Sarvodaya movement in independent India took this faltering beginning to what appeared to be its logical end.

Lord Charles Cornwallis (1732-1805) was India's Governor-General from 1786 to 1793. He is credited with introducing a number of reforms. Many of those reforms were recommended by Charles Grant and Henry Dundas, the head of the East India Company. They laid the foundation of "The Settlement" to reform the revenue and land system of Bengal. The reforms did not work out as intended. They were the sort of steps taken by Moses' protégé and successor, Joshua, 1,400 years before Christ. In short, the Pitts-Cornwallis reforms attempted to introduce the Bible's concept of property rights into feudal India.

The idea of agricultural property rights laid the foundation of India's later developments; however, land reforms did not initially succeed because they went against Bengal's socio-economic culture. Historian Percival Spear points out that for all practical reasons, the settlements could not be made with individual farmers. They had to be made with the zamindars: aristocrats with inherited positions. They held large tracts of land and had the responsibility to collect a fixed amount of taxes for the Company and the Mughal Empire. The hope was that the Permanent Settlement of Bengal would incentivise zamindars to invest surplus income in increasing production. However, the well-intentioned attempt to give Biblical-style secure property rights to zamindars failed to improve the land and cultivation. The initial implementation failed partly because the zamindars became the new nawabs. They squeezed revenue out of the tenants but did not reinvest it in the land. Percival Spear notes that, "The great difficulty of the Company was to know how much the countryside could safely pay. This was the zamindar's secret, which they were disinclined to share since their living depended on its exploitation."

The Permanent Settlement of Bengal failed partly because Indian zamindars invested the surplus income to make their lives in Calcutta more convenient, even luxurious. They did little to improve the lot of their fellow men, the cultivators. Nevertheless, introducing the Bible's concept of secure property rights for the poorest tiller of the soil became a significant first step in building India into a relatively just society.

The attempt to bring the Bible's idea of land ownership into Bengal inspired social reformers such as Keshab Chandra Sen (1838-1884). He realised that in order to change culture, our people needed more than learned discourses on ancient Hindu scriptures. Bengal needed more than pious rituals of Telugu Brahmins reciting Vedas in Brahmo Samaj meetings. Sen went on to introduce into the Brahmo Samaj the Bible's emphasis on repentance and prayer.

This biblical understanding of spirituality impacted Nobel Laureate Rabindranath Tagore (1861–1941). His family's wealth had come from the zamindari system. Jesus' Sermon on the Mount made him renounce that exploitative system. In one of his poems in Gitanjali, Tagore summarised Christ's beatitudes: "You are there with the poorest and the meekest; you are always there with the helpless people—I adore you, my God, amongst them."

The Bible's impact on Tagore went much deeper than poetic imagination. He learnt that biblical repentance required restitution. Therefore, he sent his son and son-in-law to America to study agriculture. In 1907, he wrote to them:

"Remember that the wealth of the zamindar is the wealth of the farmer—in reality, it is the starving farmer who is financing your education. Upon your return, you have the full responsibility to repay this debt rather than pursuing your own prosperity. "

Since Sam Higginbottom was also trying to transform India's exploitative agrarian culture. Tagore recognised the value of Higgenbottom's mission. He followed the example of several Maharajas and contacted Higginbottom to design his educational work in Shantiniketan in such a way that it would change Indian culture at the grassroots.

Madan Mohan Malviya's Banaras Hindu University, Tagore's Shantiniketan, and Mahatma Gandhi's Bunyadi Shiksha (Basic Education) testify to the Bible's profound impact on Indian culture. They were radically different from anything Hindu gurus had done earlier. These leaders of modern India became a new breed of gurus who opened their hearts to the Bible. Gandhi's vision of Sarvodaya, carried forward by Acharya Vinoba Bhave and Jai Prakash Narayan, was directly inspired by Christ's teaching. What we do for "the least" and "the last" of the poor (Dalits, oppressed ones) is done unto God. It is because of the Bible that Sarvodaya (upliftment of all) has now become Antyodaya (upliftment of the last). The Lord Jesus taught that principle in Matthew 25:31–46.

To sum up this section: Hindu and Muslim rulers never gave rights to property and education to Indian women and Shudras. Furthermore, colonialism had no reason to do so. The idea of such rights came to us from the Bible. They have prepared the ground for developing India's potential. The next need is to teach our people to obey God and not covet and steal their neighbours' produce or intellectual properties. That ethical change will make it possible for our youth to dream, invent, innovate, and make India one of the greatest nations in the world.

Character: From Covetousness to Creativity

The upper castes in our villages were upset that the lower castes were going to Punjab to harvest, partly because that made it very difficult for them to get labourers for their fields. Their culture had not taught them that to work with their hands was noble. Hindu, Muslim, and British rulers had never felt any need to change India's poor work ethic.

Why did Tagore want his family to repay peasants? What made Premchand condemn usury? Exacting debilitating interest from the poor was a fundamental aspect of India's stagnant economic culture. It made the rich richer without having to work hard. Reformers such as Tagore and Premchand criticised their culture because the Bible condemns covetousness as sin. God commands in Exodus 22:25, "If you lend money to any of my people with you who are poor, you shall not be like a moneylender to him, and you shall not exact interest from him."

How can we transform a covetous character into a charitable one? Why should a person create wealth and share it with the needy instead of building palaces and temples? Modernising India at this level meant replacing moneylenders with banks; promoting investment and wise philanthropy—not just charity.

The Bank of Bombay, established in 1720, became India's first joint-stock bank. Banking helped transform our exploitative and stagnant economy into a developing one. People were able to borrow money not simply to meet a family crisis but in order to invest in creative ideas and profitable projects.

Banking could not even be imagined in earlier ages when South Asia was fragmented into many kingdoms. What if a person borrows money in one princely state and disappears into another? Uniting India under one legal system made banking possible. Opposing usury and replacing moneylenders with banks was a major ethical/legal move towards modernisation. A brief discussion of the work ethic will be sufficient for now to illustrate the point that it was the Bible, not Britain, that modernised India.

The Bible's Work Ethic

Meditation and magic, yoga and occult powers (*siddhis*) glamorised in Kumbh Melas do not create wealth; work does. The Bible reveals a God who works! Creation does not spring from God's navel-gazing or sages meditating in caves. Genesis 1 tells us that God worked in order to create the cosmos. To work is godliness or god-likeness. That is why the Apostle Paul wrote in the Bible that whoever does not work should not eat (2 Thessalonians 3:10).

Mahatma Gandhi had several reasons for advocating the spinning wheel (charkha) as a panacea for Indian culture. One of his objectives was to inject the Bible's work ethic into India.

Sociologist Max Weber was Gandhi's contemporary. He presented the case that the Bible's work ethic explains why Protestant nations developed more than other countries in Europe. The reformers required Christians to study the Bible. It not only taught that God was a worker. It also taught that God created Adam and Eve to work in the Garden of Eden. They were blessed to multiply and go beyond the garden to fill the earth in order to steward the whole earth as God's children.

Mahatma Gandhi realised the necessity of injecting the Bible's idea of the nobility of manual work into India's caste-conscious culture. Therefore, he asked his high-caste followers to spin thread—a job that Hinduism had assigned to the low caste. In this regard, Mahatma Gandhi belonged to the second or third generation of Indians who imbibed the

Bible's work ethic. Promoting the use of the spinning wheel was one of the main means Gandhi used to introduce the Bible's work ethic into Indian culture.

Gandhi's success was limited. It was not easy to transform a religious culture that disdained work—especially manual and menial work—like cleaning toilets. Doing the sweeper's work became one of his major conflicts with his wife in his ashram in South Africa. India remains one of the dirtiest countries in the world. Not many Prime Ministers and presidents sweep their streets in front of cameras in order to teach their nations that cleaning streets is a virtue.

Whatever his other faults and failures, Gandhiji succeeded in inspiring his close followers to engage in purposeful social work. Nehruji, for example, rejected Gandhi's opposition to industrialisation, but he accepted the work ethic. As Prime Minister, Nehru kept a stanza from Robert Frost's poem close to his heart. He copied this stanza with his own hand:

The woods are lovely, dark and deep,
But I have promises to keep,
And miles to go before I sleep,
And miles to go before I sleep.

Failed reforms discourage further efforts, but faith sustains the reformers' confidence in progress. Faith, in turn, is renewed by regular reading of the Bible. In difficult times, it was the Bible's revelation of the Saviour God that inspired Mahatma Gandhi to sing,

"Lead, kindly Light, amidst the encircling gloom...
Lead Thou me on!
The night is dark and I am far from home,
Lead Thou me on!
Keep Thou my feet; I do not ask to see...
The distant scene - one step enough for me."

This, one of Gandhi's favourite hymns, was written by the sick and tearful John Henry Newman when he was stranded in Italy in 1833. That was the same year in which Lord Macaulay persuaded the British

Parliament to govern India in a moral way. He knew that India's political trajectory was unpredictable. Why the urgency? Macaulay's aspiration was that Indians may learn to govern themselves as a free nation.

Newman titled his poem "*The Pillar and the Cloud.*" It was a direct reference to the Exodus saga of God's pillar of cloud guiding rebellious Jews out of slavery in Egypt, through the wilderness, and into the Promised Land. Most of the reforms that Moses instituted ended in terrible wickedness. Failure and sin brought God's judgment upon the Jews. Yet the God who laid judgments upon human folly, also offered hope of forgiveness and renewal based on national repentance.

Human wickedness corrupts every good law and institution. Keshab Chandra Sen's contemporary, Mahatma Jotiba Phule, knew it was the wickedness of kulkarnis and zamindars that had ruined British efforts to transform Indian agriculture. This convinced him that spiritual regeneration had to accompany good policies and administrative reforms. Phule wrote,

Now at least our [British] government should wake up and place at least one English or Scottish preacher in each village, gifting him one plot of tenantless land for his upkeep, and assign him the task of preaching and submitting to the government at least one report every year on everything that happens in the village.

Sam Higginbottom, as pointed out in an earlier chapter, founded Asia's best agricultural institute on a theology of *The Gospel and the Plow*. He realised that spiritual transformation must go hand in hand with education, science, and technology. That will make India into a developing nation. Education and technology were needed to transform agriculture, but transforming character, including an attitude inclined to hard work, was an equally important mission. Higginbottom wrote:

"Whatever might have been our experiences and efforts, we could not get away from the idea that there would be no kingdom of God in India without an amelioration of poverty and that this must be founded on a more productive agriculture. This conviction dominated all that we said and did."

Higginbottom promoted agriculture and technology. But he knew that the gospel was necessary for transforming our character:

> "On one point in our discussion, the students [of economics] were unanimous. Methods of improving life in the villages were not their business. Everything was the fault of the government, and all reform, therefore, was the government's responsibility. I pointed out to them that the chief exploiters of the villager were the petty government officials. They answered that the government should appoint better men. I asked where the government could secure these better men. The students were at a loss to know."

The Bible sustained the reformers' slow and steady progress towards making India into a society where biblical justice could replace *Manusmriti* (Laws of Manu, the Hindu Code); modern banking could destroy debilitating usury; the development of vernaculars could empower aam aadmi (the common man); technology could free us from caste-based slavery; women could be emancipated to help pull our national "bullock cart"; education could be universalised; a free press and free elections could check the abuse of power. Each of these topics deserves detailed studies. They are needed to help future generations appreciate the Bible's role in shaping our developing nation.

Chapter 8

The Bible and India's Independence

The Story of India's Independence

India was a British colony. On 15 August 1947, it gained independence without fighting a war. How did that happen?

I grew up hearing the story of India's independence. The British East India Company began colonising Bengal after winning the battles of Plassey (1757) and Buxar (1764). The First War of India's Independence began, I was told, a hundred years later, on May 10, 1857. A group of Indian soldiers serving in the British army in Meerut killed arrogant British officers, marched to Delhi, and declared Bahadur Shah II as India's Mughal Emperor. More Indian soldiers and nobility joined the revolt, but a much smaller British army crushed it.

The British Crown disbanded the East India Company and began to rule India. After World War I, Mahatma Gandhi began a non-violent movement to liberate India from British rule. On August 8, 1942, Gandhi and the Congress Working Committee launched a peaceful movement asking the British to "Quit India." The next day, British rulers arrested Mahatma Gandhi and most of his important followers. Many of the freedom fighters were released only in 1945 at the end of World War II, and yet the British decided to give India independence. They withdrew peacefully.

The story did not make sense. Therefore, it was natural to inquire: if the British came to loot India, if they were able to beat Germany and Japan, if they defeated Subhash Chandra Bose's Indian National Army and had no problem keeping non-violent "freedom fighters" imprisoned, why did they leave? Why did India fail to produce a Mahatma Gandhi during the seven centuries of the Muslim rule in Delhi?

No one answered such questions. Everyone simply repeated the same story that I had already heard many times. Therefore, I decided to investigate the history of India's independence. That research helped me realise that the Bible was the force that liberated India from British rule.

The Background

Thirty-six years before Mahatma Gandhi was born, 23 years before Bal Gangadhar Tilak was born, and 24 before the Revolt of 1857—that is, in 1833, the British Parliament had already accepted the duty that liberating India was Britain's moral duty to God. That case for wisdom was argued by Thomas Babington Macaulay. He persuaded the British Parliament that India should be governed in a way that would prepare her to govern herself.

Macaulay's brother-in-law, Charles Trevelyan (1807-1886), came to India as an evangelical civil servant. He argued that the purpose of Christian education was not to train Indians to sustain colonial rule but to prepare them to govern their own land. Such a mission was not palatable to many colonial rulers. They resisted the Bible-inspired campaign to educate India for liberty. However, Bible-obeying Christians persisted and succeeded in bringing modern universities into India. Their goal was clear: prepare young people to govern India with justice, liberty, and righteousness.

Before any Indian asked for independence, Trevelyan was unequivocal in his 1838 book, *On the Education of the People of India*:

> "The existing connexion between two such distant countries as England and India, cannot, in the nature of things, be permanent: no effort of policy can prevent the natives from ultimately regaining their independence. But there are two ways of arriving at this point. One of these is through the medium of revolution, the other through that of reform. . . [Revolution] must end in the complete alienation of mind and separation of interests between ourselves and the natives; the other [reform] in a permanent alliance, founded on mutual

benefit and good will. The only means at our disposal for preventing [revolution] and securing... the results [of reform] is to set the natives on a process of European improvement. The natives will have independence, after first learning how to make use of it, and we shall exchange profitable subjects for still more profitable allies... trained by us to happiness and independence, and endowed with our learning and political institutions, India will remain the proudest monument of British benevolence..."

Did colonialism motivate Macaulay to become a champion of India's freedom? Or did Hinduism teach him to become a spokesman for liberty?

Three centuries before Macaulay and Trevelyan, German reformer Martin Luther had expounded the Bible in *A Treatise Concerning Christian Liberty* in 1520. Luther's treatise was the opposite of Machiavelli's *The Prince* (1532), a perspective on politics as the pursuit of power. Every Bible reader knew that the Bible began to be written down after God sent Moses to Egypt to liberate Hebrews from slavery. The Old Testament was penned for the freedom of a nation.

That is not to say that Jews and Christians never used religion to justify slavery. They did. Jesus, himself a Jew, described the religious leaders as slave-makers (Luke 11:46; Matthew 23). He told the Jews that religion enslaves, but truth liberates: "If you remain in my word, you will know the truth, and the truth will set you free." (John 8:31–32). Likewise, the Apostle Paul's epistle to the Galatians argued that not only Jewish leaders but also some of the Jewish followers of Christ were out to enslave fellow Christians. (Galatians 4:21-5:11).

In his book, Trevelyan explained that education (truth) was the means to prepare India for independence. On July 26, 1833, Macaulay challenged Parliament with these words [I have inserted some paraphrasing].

"Are we to keep the people of India ignorant, in order that we may keep them submissive? [That is what Brahminism had done.] Or do we think that we can give them knowledge without awakening ambition? Or, do we mean to awaken ambition [for independence] and provide it with no legitimate vent? ... The path of duty [to God] is plain to us; it is also the path of wisdom, of national prosperity, of national honour.

"The destinies of our Indian empire are covered with thick darkness. It is difficult to form any conjecture as to the fate reserved for a state which resembles no other in history . . . the laws which regulate its growth and decay are still unknown to us. It may be that the public mind of India may expand under our system till it has outgrown that system, that by good governance we may educate our subjects into a capacity for better government; that having become instructed in European knowledge, they may in some future age, demand European institutions. Whether such a day will ever come, I know not. But never will I attempt to avert or to retard it. Whenever it comes [whenever Indians ask us to 'Quit India'], it will be the proudest day in English history. To have found a great people sunk in the lowest depths of slavery and superstition [of Hinduism and Islam] to have so ruled them as to have made them desirous and capable of all the privileges of citizens would indeed be a title to glory all our own. The sceptre may pass away from us. Unforeseen accidents may derange our most profound schemes of policy. Victory may be inconstant to our arms. But there are triumphs which are followed by no reverses. There is an empire [God's kingdom] exempt from all natural causes of decay. Those triumphs are the pacific triumphs of reason over barbarism, that empire is the imperishable empire of our arts and our morals, our literature and our laws [if they reflect God's will on earth]."

Twenty-five years later, the British established universities in Calcutta, Madras, and Bombay. But how was this Bible-inspired vision of India's independence realised in 1947? What role did Gandhi and Congress play in ending colonial rule? I've discussed some of that history in earlier books. The First World War enabled British leaders like Edwin Montague to put India's independence on the front burner, beginning the chain reaction that catapulted Mahatma Gandhi into leadership. Instead of repeating that history, allow me to recap the Bible's role in promoting national sovereignty, which ended European imperialism and secured India's independence.

The Bible's Idea of 'Nation' Won the West

Some complex civilisations, such as the Minoans, had existed in small pockets of Europe before Alexander the Great (356 BC-323 BC) united tribal societies and city-states to create the first European empire. Just before the birth of Jesus, Rome consolidated that imperial spirit of subjugating others through wars.

Imperialism and wars go hand in hand. The wars that threatened the very concept of the Holy Roman Empire were the religious wars triggered by the Protestant Reformation. The most consequential of these was the Thirty Years' War from 1618 to 1648, which ended with the Peace of Westphalia. That "peace" introduced the Bible's concept of "nation" as an alternative to Europe's idea of empire. Theologians had baptised that pagan idea of empire as "Christendom"—Christ's kingdom.

The Peace of Westphalia concluded with recognising the Netherlands and Switzerland as sovereign nation-states, like ancient Israel, independent of the Holy Roman Empire.

Pagan empires, including Islamic Caliphates, do not respect national borders. Hinduism had turned the imperialistic expansion of one's kingdom into a religious ritual called "Ashwamedh Yajna" (the Horse Sacrifice). In contrast, the Bible taught that God's idea of peace on earth involved creating sovereignnation-states, governing themselves, in their own languages, in defined territories. This view began in Genesis 10-12 and developed in books from Exodus to Joshua. The Apostle Paul summed it up in a speech in Athens.

"From one man he [God] made all the nations, that they should inhabit the whole earth; and he marked out their appointed times in history and the boundaries of their lands.

God did this so that they would seek him and perhaps reach out for him and find him, though he is not far from any one of us." (Acts 17: 26-27)

Imperialism was so deeply embedded in Europe's soul that it could not be ended with the Peace of 1648. Nevertheless, the Bible brought the idea of national sovereignty across the ocean to the thirteen British colonies in North America. The First Great (Spiritual) Awakening between 1732 and 1770 opened the Christian mind to follow the example of the Netherlands. The American colonies began their own successful revolution against British imperialism in 1775. Their Christian heritage prevented them from becoming thirteen kingdoms, or a new empire, out to colonise Canada and Mexico. The Bible united the colonies to become a sovereign nation—a champion of liberty. The American Revolution inspired the French Revolution (1789–99), Napoleon's dictatorship (1799–1815), and the Latin American revolutions (1811–1830s). These ended the Holy Roman Empire but not Europe's imperial spirit.

Atlantic Charter to End Europe's Christian Colonialism

Europe's colonialism ended with World War II in 1945. The Soviet Union's Communist colonialism continued until 1991. Not just India, but practically every colony became independent, even if most of them had not been educated to govern themselves. Gandhi's laudable "non-violence" was not the moral force that forced Prime Minister Winston Churchill to end imperialism. What compelled Britain and France (as well as Holland, Germany, Spain, Portugal, and Japan) was the Atlantic Charter. This agreement between British Prime Minister Winston Churchill and American President Franklin D. Roosevelt was announced on 14 August 1941.

Elliott Roosevelt, son of President Roosevelt, was an eyewitness to all but three of the eleven meetings Roosevelt had with Churchill during World War II. In his book *As He Saw It* (1946), Elliott describes one of those meetings. It was the climax of the conversation about colonialism between Churchill and his father:

"Churchill had got up to walk about the room. Talking, gesticulating, at length he paused in front of Father, was silent for a moment, looking at him, and then brandished a stubby forefinger under Father's nose.

'Mr. President,' he cried, 'I believe you are trying to do away with the British Empire. Every idea you entertain about the structure of the postwar world demonstrates it. But in spite of that—and his forefinger waved— 'in spite of that, we know that you constitute our only hope. And—his voice sank dramatically—you know that we know it. You know that we know that without America, the Empire won't stand.' "

In that moment, Churchill admitted that victory and peace could only be won according to precepts which the United States of America would lay down. And in saying what he did, he was acknowledging that British colonial policy would be dead. British attempts to dominate world trade would be dead. And British ambitions to play off the U.S.S.R. against the USA would also be dead.

The eight-point Atlantic Charter ensured that after the war was over, Allied victors would create the United Nations, not the "United Empires." The third of the eight points committed the USA and Britain to respect every colony's right to self-determination. Even after agreeing to the charter, Churchill wanted to give that right only to people colonised by Germany, not to British colonies. Yet, given Roosevelt's resolve, the charter had already created ripples that became the tsunami that swept aside the hesitations of British colonialists such as Churchill.

The American opinion on national independence and self-determination was the fruit of the strong theological debates that resulted in the Peace of Augsburg in 1555 between Lutherans and Roman Catholics, and in 1648 in the Peace of Westphalia among Calvinists, Lutherans, and Roman Catholics. It was the American theological understanding of national independence that enabled Roosevelt to dismantle the British Empire.

Roosevelt knew the Bible and expounded it in his speeches. In one of his most famous speeches on D-Day, the landing of the Allied troops on the Normandy Beach in France to engage the Germans, Roosevelt gave a prayer in which he invoked "Almighty God" to lead the Allied troops who had set out to "preserve our Republic, our religion, and our civilisation and to set free a suffering humanity." Roosevelt asked for God's blessing, knowing that "their road will be long and hard." Later in his prayer, Roosevelt asked for God's help in conquering "the apostles of greed and racial arrogances." Roosevelt sought with "our sister nations" to move the world into "unity that will spell a sure peace, a peace invulnerable to the schemings of unworthy men, and a peace that will let all men live in freedom, reaping the just rewards of their honest toil."

Roosevelt concluded with a phrase from the Lord's Prayer found in the Bible: "Thy will be done."

Earlier, in August 1941, when Churchill stepped off the battleship HMS Prince of Wales onto Roosevelt's "fishing boat," USS Augusta, a US Navy cruiser, he was not merely a global hero. He was also the chief politico of history's largest empire and the war leader of the free world. By contrast, Roosevelt was simply the president of a nation on the margins of global geopolitics, a nation hesitant to join the war.

The two men had not met before, even though they had corresponded about drawing America into the war since 1939. Churchill may have been desperate because he feared that a victorious Germany could colonise Britain.

Elliott Roosevelt's memoirs of the conversation between Roosevelt and Churchill tell us what transpired in those meetings. Elliott recalls that his father said,

" '...after the war, one of the preconditions of any lasting peace will have to be the greatest possible freedom of trade.'

He paused. The PM's head was lowered; he was watching Father steadily, from under one eyebrow.

'No artificial barriers,' Father pursued. 'As few favoured economic agreements as possible. Opportunities for expansion. Markets open for healthy competition.' His eye wandered innocently around the room.

Churchill shifted in his armchair. 'The British Empire trade agreements,' he began heavily, 'are—'

Father broke in. 'Yes. Those Empire trade agreements are a case in point. It's because of them that the people of India and Africa, of all the colonial Near East and Far East, are still as backward as they are.'

Churchill's neck reddened, and he crouched forward. 'Mr. President, England does not propose for a moment to lose its favoured position among the British Dominions. The trade that has made England great shall continue, and under conditions prescribed by England's ministers.'

'You see,' said Father slowly, 'it is along in here somewhere that there is likely to be some disagreement between you, Winston, and me. I am firmly of the belief that if we are to arrive at a stable peace, it must involve the development of backward countries. Backward peoples. How can this be done? It can't be done, obviously, by eighteenth-century methods. Now—'

'Who's talking eighteenth-century methods?'

'Whichever of your ministers recommends a policy which takes wealth in raw materials out of a colonial country but which returns nothing to the people of that country in consideration. Twentieth-century methods involve bringing industry to these colonies. Twentieth-century methods include increasing the wealth of a people by increasing their standard of living, by educating them, by bringing them sanitation—by making sure that they get a return for the raw wealth of their community.'

Around the room, all of us were leaning forward attentively. [One of Roosevelt's closest advisers, Harry Lloyd] Hopkins was grinning. Commander Thompson, Churchill's aide, was looking glum and alarmed. The PM himself was beginning to look apoplectic.

"You mentioned India,' he growled. 'Yes. I can't believe that we can fight a war against fascist slavery and at the same time not work to free people all over the world from a backward colonial policy.'"

It should not be difficult to grasp why Indian historians do not tell us about America's critical role in India's independence. Establishment historians had a vested interest in crediting the party in power: Congress party. For some historians, it was far too embarrassing to admit that America—then a Christian capitalist country—was not interested in looting the world by teaming up with Britain. Hindutva historians want to explode the myths that support the Congress Party. Their *swadeshi* (indigenous) predisposition makes it hard for them to confess the truth that it was the USA, whose understanding of "nation" had been shaped by the Bible, that persuaded another "Christian" country (England), to give up its pagan (Roman) concept of empire.

Ultimately, it was the force of moral persuasion that dismantled the British Empire, starting with its crown jewel, India. In 1942, Mahatma Gandhi did ask the British to "Quit India." That appeal was his response to a theological "right to self-determination" agreed to in the Atlantic Charter over a year earlier. Mahatma Gandhi was also championing an alternative to Subhash Chandra Bose's proposal that only violence would lead India to independence. The right of nations to govern themselves, i.e., "self-determination," goes back to Genesis 11. That was a central point of Exodus, Joshua, and the historical books of the Old Testament. European theologians began to understand and accept that idea of national sovereignty as early as 1555. In 1648, the Peace of Westphalia reiterated that biblical idea of national sovereignty, thereby undermining the medieval idea of the Holy Roman Empire.

The foregoing is not meant to ignore Mahatma Gandhi's role in India's independence, although I am implying that his role has been exaggerated by establishment historians. Many of them seem to think that the end of colonialism equals freedom. Mahatma Gandhi is important because he transformed the elitist Indian National Congress into a mass-based political movement. That made it possible for the British to hand over India's governance to the leaders elected by the people of India and Pakistan.

The three Round Table Conferences were held between 1930 and 1932 to discuss colonial India's future. They exposed that India's independence was delayed by her own leaders, their vested interests, and mutual dislike.

The British had won South Asia from the Mughals and a thousand other maharajas. Should their states be returned to them? That would mean a return to feudalism. Indian leaders could not agree on who should govern India after the British left. Nor was it clear how independent India could ensure that liberty reaches every Indian.

Inspired and supported by a retired British civil servant, Allan Octavian Hume, the Indian National Congress was founded in 1885. It was an organisation of university-educated elitist Indians. They organised conferences to pass resolutions on how the British should give more authority to Indians. No one had elected "the Congress." It did not represent the common people. Nor did it have any historic or moral claim to govern India.

As I have pointed out in *India: The Grand Experiment*, in 1895, some Congress leaders decided to allow the lower caste spokesmen of the *Social Conference* to use the Congress platform to oppose their enslavement by upper caste Hindus. In response, Bal Gangadhar Tilak's followers threatened to burn down the Congress *Pandal* (tent), if Hindu customs were opposed from that platform. Congress uninvited the *Social Conference*.

Later, in 1917, when the British announced their post-World War intention to give Home-Rule to India, Congress attempted to bring the "Depressed Classes" under its political umbrella. It passed false resolutions on behalf of the lower castes in order to deceive the British.

Thoughtful lower caste leaders came together in Bombay under the chairmanship of Bapuji Namdeo Bagade to condemn Congress. They declared that the castes crushed by Hindus would rather remain under British rule than be governed by the upper caste elite. Some of the resolutions passed included:

1. Resolution of loyalty to the British throne.

2. That this meeting cannot give support to the Congress-(Muslim) League scheme, in spite of it having been declared to have been passed at the meeting on the 11th November 1917 by an overwhelming majority.

3. That it is the sense of this meeting that the administration of India should be largely under the control of the British till all classes, and especially the Depressed Classes, rise up to a condition of effectively participating in the administration of the country.

Dr. Bhimrao Ambedkar summed up the strong sentiments expressed in such resolutions in his book *Annihilation of Caste* (1936). He wrote, "*Swarajya* (Independence) has got no significance without establishing a casteless society." He knew that colonial "political brutality is nothing when compared with the social brutality" of the Hindu social order.

Who should govern an independent India? The descendants of former Hindu, Muslim, and Sikh rulers wanted their kingdoms returned to them. But Muslims did not trust Hindus. Hindus had never treated the lower castes, the "Untouchables," as Hindus. They were not allowed to enter Hindu temples, read Hindu scriptures, eat with Hindus, or marry their children. Consequently, they did not want an elitist Indian National Congress to govern India.

That distrust climaxed in the Gandhi-Ambedkar conflict during the Second Round Table Conference (1931). Mahatma Gandhi tried to present himself as the sole representative of the Hindus, including those crushed by Hindu society, the Dalits. Dr. Ambedkar argued that the Untouchables were not Hindus but Hinduism's victims. This truth had been forcefully presented by Mahatma Jotiba Phule in his book *Slavery* (1873). The Simon Commission documented it officially in 1928. Therefore, no one accepted Mahatma Gandhi's false claim.

What could independent India do to liberate Hinduism's slaves? The answer was obvious: the Untouchables (also known as scheduled castes) and tribals (known as scheduled tribes) must be given the right to elect their own legislators. Mahatma Gandhi objected to this solution because he foresaw the long-term implications: political interests would reinforce the chasm that already existed between the upper and lower castes. The untouchable castes would quit Hinduism.

Therefore, Gandhiji argued that some constituencies should be reserved exclusively for the Scheduled Castes and Tribes. In those constituencies, they would be the only candidates for the elections to the Federal Parliament and State legislative assemblies. However, all citizens would vote to elect representatives from among them. Dr. Ambedkar rejected this proposal because its implication was clear: several lower caste candidates, with limited resources, will run for office. The lower caste votes will be divided. Candidates dedicated to serving the interests of the upper castes will win because they will have the financial resources to contest elections.

The Second Round Table Conference failed to resolve the conflict. Therefore, it authorised the Prime Minister to resolve the matter. In August 1932, Prime Minister Ramsay McDonald announced his Communal Award, supporting Dr. Ambedkar's view that the Untouchables should elect their own leaders. This is exactly what Moses had done 3,500 years earlier: ask each tribe to elect the leaders they knew and respected. Moses could have appointed leaders who were loyal to him. But governance is effective if people choose their leaders and hold them accountable.

Mahatma Gandhi rejected a policy that would have empowered the downtrodden and began a "fast unto death." His followers warned Dr. Ambedkar that if Gandhi died, his followers would hold Ambedkar responsible. And who knows what they might do to unarmed, vulnerable untouchables? By saving Gandhi's life, Ambedkar might, in fact, save the lives of the downtrodden he was trying to save.

Dr. Ambedkar signed the "Poona Pact" against his better judgment. This was blackmail because the Pact was won by force, not truth and reason. Through the Poona Pact, Gandhiji gave Hindus the fig leaf to cover their shame of slavery. That fig leaf, wrote Manyavar Kanshi Ram, began *The Chamcha Age* (1982). It turned Scheduled Caste (SC) and Scheduled Tribe (ST) elected leaders into the stooges of upper caste politicians. Nevertheless, the Poona Pact allowed the British to write the India Act of 1935 and paved the way for India's independence and its Constitution.

Did Mahatma Gandhi want the upliftment of the untouchables? There is no reason to doubt his personal sincerity. However, his personal commitment to Sarvodaya—upliftment of all—came from Christ, not from Hinduism. His political followers did not follow his spirit because it was alien to their culture.

Kanshiram and his Bahujan Samaj Party (BSP) for Dalits removed the fig leaves. They took the lower caste votes away from the Congress Party. Dr. Ambedkar thought that quitting Hinduism and converting to Neo-Buddhism might give a new religious identity to the Dalits. Kanshiram explored that option by establishing a Buddhist Research Center in New Delhi. His research failed to convince him that Buddhism could make the difference that Ambedkar had hoped for. Even so, at the end of his life, Kanshiram did want to convert to Buddhism, but illness prevented him from doing so.

The political decline of Congress and the BSP made it possible for the Hindutva movement to try to unify the higher and lower castes. It has attempted to unite them by creating a common enemy: Islam. This strategy for forging unity based on hatred has had limited political success. The unity is falling apart because, while the upper castes regard the Constitution as anti-Hindu, the lower castes and Muslims see it as their relative safeguard against the militant ideology of Hindutva. To that topic, therefore, we should now turn.

Chapter 9

The Bible and the Soul of Modern India

Hindutva's father, Veer Savarkar, was right: "There is nothing Indian about the Indian Constitution." The very idea that a nation should run on the basis of a written constitution (covenant) and just laws came from the Bible.

When Joshua succeeded Moses as Israel's leader, God commanded him, "Keep this book of the law always on your lips; meditating on it day and night, so that you may be careful to do everything written in it." (Joshua 1:8). Further, "And when [the king] sits on the throne of his kingdom, he shall write for himself in a book a copy of this law." (Deuteronomy 17:18).

The Huguenots (French Calvinists) introduced the Jewish idea of a national covenant, or constitution, into Europe after 1572. Scottish Reformers applied that idea to church organisations. Ordinary church members, not bishops, began to elect elders, who then chose national leaders and held them accountable in the light of a codified book of rules.

Presbyterians brought the Scottish experiment to the United States. Their written constitution united into one denomination the many Presbyterian churches scattered in North American colonies. About two-thirds of the American Founding Fathers were Calvinists, and a majority of them were Presbyterians. The Founders applied the system developed by the Presbyterian Church to the government of this new country.

India's Constituent Assembly relied on aspects of the American Constitution as it expanded the India Act of 1935. That Act, the basis and forerunner of our Constitution, was written by British civil servants.

British rulers and civil servants had to create India's constitutional framework because the Indian National Congress rejected "The Commonwealth of India Bill, 1925," drafted by the Annie Besant Committee. That Committee was led by legal luminaries such as Sir Tej Bahadur Sapru. The Congress then appointed its own (Motilal) Nehru Committee in 1928 to draft its proposal for a Constitution to govern India. Tej Bahadur Sapru served as one of the most experienced legal minds on this Committee as well. The Muslim League, however, rejected the "Nehru Report," which was the Constitution proposed by the Congress.

The following year, Muhammad Ali Jinnah presented the Muslim League's "Fourteen Points," outlining how India should govern itself. The Congress rejected the Muslim League's proposal! These proposals and the reports of the three Round Table Conferences formed the background of the India Act of 1935. That Act became the basis of the 1950 Constitution of modern India.

This Constitution has been governing India since 1950. The problem is that the Hindutva movement never accepted India's Constitution. Many Indians think that the Constitution is just another book, one to be edited or modified at will. Since coming to power, the party of Hindutva (Bharatiya Janata Party, BJP) has wanted to change the Constitution through peaceful, democratic means. That hope is now fading. This has raised a sobering question: could Hindutva use force to overthrow a Constitution which it regards as anti-Hindu?

A number of analysts today assert that the BJP has turned India into a "banana republic"—a corrupt and misgoverned country. Public institutions—intelligence agencies, police, courts, the Income Tax Enforcement Directorate, nationalised banks—that exist to serve the citizens are blatantly abused to harass individuals, businesses, and opposition politicians.

Where do bananas come from? A child may think that the fruit on his dining table comes from the market. Adults know that fruit grows on trees and plants. Growing good fruit takes much care and effort. The Constituent Assembly did not purchase India's magnificent Constitution from a market of constitutions. They debated and carefully chose the best available ideas to unite widely divergent cultures to create a potentially great nation. Writing India's Constitution was an exercise in forging the soul of modern India—different from traditional cultures.

Here let us discuss a fundamental question: Is the Constitution just another book, or is there something sacred about it?

Is the Constitution Sacred?

"Low" caste Indians are passionate about the Constitution because it makes them equal to the "high" castes and grants them reservations (quotas) in the sectors of education, government jobs, and legislative bodies. The same fact makes some high-caste people want to throw out the Constitution. They argue that the Reservation system undermines merit and quality. The controversy keeps the discussion at a pragmatic level—is the Constitution good or bad for a specific sector of society? Moral principles behind the Constitution are rarely debated.

Pragmatic debates about the usefulness of the Constitution necessarily boil down to a question of power. Democracy—one person, one vote—gives power to the lower castes and tribes because they happen to be the majority. Should the higher castes then use force to end democracy and undo the system that favours the majority, i.e., the lower castes?

Those who advocate throwing out democracy often use China as an example. China, they say, has surpassed India in most fields because it has a non-democratic, authoritarian system of government. The naysayers of democracy assert that India can also progress, if we discard the democratic Constitution we borrowed from the West. Clearly, it does not suit our corrupt Asian society.

For various reasons, most politicians, civil servants, police, courts, and public institutions cannot actually say out loud what they think and believe. They pay lip service to the Constitution, even though they undermine it in practice.

Former Prime Minister Justin Trudeau of Canada accused India's Hindu government of using its diplomats to hire criminals to murder a Canadian citizen. Likewise, former US President Joe Biden's administration also accused the BJP government of hiring criminals in an attempt to kill an American citizen. Pakistan is condemning India for sending mercenaries to Pakistan to kill Pakistani citizens.

I am inclined to believe these accusations because of my own experience in 1980. The District Magistrate of Chhatarpur unjustly banned my effort to organise relief for farmers affected by a hailstorm in Madhya Pradesh. I submitted to the District Magistrate's ban respectfully and instead invited the hailstorm victims to gather in the premises of the Gandhi Ashram for a non-sectarian prayer meeting. We wanted them to ask God to provide relief. He could move the government itself to have compassion where it had none.

Instead, the police superintendent sent a jeep to bring me to his bungalow. At his home, he ordered me to cancel the prayer meeting. If I did not call the meeting off, he warned me, "I will personally kill you. I will not arrest you or present you before a magistrate. I will take you from your home into the jungle and shoot you. Hyenas will eat your body. Are you going to cancel that prayer meeting?"

"Sir," I replied, "Before making that decision, I will need to ask my wife if she is willing to be a widow."

The superintendent realised that I was not taking him seriously. That was true. I did not think that a high-ranking police officer who had taken an oath to uphold the Constitution of India would murder an innocent social worker. To convince me that he meant business, he spent the better part of the next hour, telling me anecdotes of the many citizens he had personally killed without any arrest or trial.

In the end, the district administration did not kill me. They threw me into jail for "disturbing the peace and tranquility of the district for daring to organise a prayer meeting. In prison, many inmates came to me narrating the tales of their imprisonment. Many of them said that the police framed them on serious but trumped-up charges such as murder or rape, simply because they had dared to campaign against candidates of the ruling political party. At that time, the Congress party was in power. Mrs. Indira Gandhi was the Prime Minister, and Arjun Singh was the Chief Minister of Madhya Pradesh. The Hindutva party came to power later. Since that time, in states across India, innocent people are harassed and arrested daily not just for political opposition to the BJP but for the crime of seeking God and praying to Jesus.

My eye-opening prison experience showed me that although politicians and police officers take their oath of office by placing their hands on the Constitution, they don't actually believe in a citizen's "fundamental rights" to life, liberty, justice, or fraternity. Our leaders and officers are unjust because they do not believe that there is anything sacred about the basic commitments of our Constitution.

Why Don't Indians Believe in the Constitution's Sanctity?

Our leaders and officers do not uphold the Constitution as sacred because our universities have deceived the nation. University professors have taught that Constitutionalism came from Rousseau's theory of the Social Contract. Jean Jacques Rousseau, an Enlightenment philosopher, lived from 1712 to 1778 and drove France into darkness. His humanist ideas influenced the disastrous French Revolution (1789–1799), which professed liberty, equality, and fraternity but instead became a Reign of Terror. It ended in Napoleon's dictatorship, which plunged Europe into seemingly endless wars.

Revolutionaries in America wrote their Constitution in 1787 and adopted it in 1788. That Constitution has remained until now. The French Revolutionaries wrote their first constitution in 1791. In 1793, 1795, 1799, 1802, 1804, 1814, 1815, 1830, 1848, 1852, 1875, 1940, 1945, 1946, and 1958, they had to rewrite new constitutions—France's constitution has been officially changed sixteen times!

Pakistan became independent at the same time as India in August 1947. It has changed its constitution three times: in 1956, 1962, and

1973. Only one of its elected governments has completed a full five-year term. Every other government has ended in assassination, coup, or military dictatorship. Our southern neighbour, Sri Lanka, has changed its constitution four times, while our northern neighbour, Nepal, has written seven constitutions since 1948. If a constitution is nothing but a social contract between people (so Rousseau asserted), why should it be considered sacred? Why shouldn't it change when contracting parties change their minds?

The United States went through a bloody Civil War from 1861 to 1865. The war, America's Constitution has remained the same for almost two and a half centuries. One important reason for this is that the American Constitution was undergirded by the Bible, as expounded by French Huguenots. In *The Book That Made Your World: How the Bible Created the Soul of Western Civilisation*, I have explained how the Huguenots derived their idea of the sanctity of Constitutionalism Two covenants are described in the Old Testament books of 2 Kings and 2 Chronicles. The first is a covenant made by the Jewish High Priest Jehoiada between God and King Joash. The second is a covenant made between the king and his people. (See 2 Kings 11 and 2 Chronicles 23). The king took an oath to serve God. Based on the king's commitment to obey God, the people took an oath to serve the king.

Rousseau and the European Enlightenment actually undermined biblical constitutionalism. The French philosopher removed the solemn covenant between God and king, reducing government to merely a social contract between the ruler and the ruled. Do people have to obey their rulers if the rulers are unfaithful to God and disobey His moral law?

Do the high values enshrined in our Constitution reflect God's moral law? Are rulers obliged to obey God? Honest answers to these questions will determine whether or not our constitutionalism will survive to make India a wise and great nation.

The Bible Changed India's Definition of Leadership

Prime Minister Jawaharlal Nehru followed the example of the Lord Jesus. Jesus taught that to be the greatest, to be the "Prime Minister," meant to be the "First Servant" of the people. Jesus washed the feet of his disciples and said to them, "You call me 'Teacher' and 'Lord' and rightly so, for that is what I am. Now that I have washed your feet, you also should wash one another's feet." (John 13:13-14)

Nehruji was a Brahmin, and the *Manusmriti* had taught that even elderly people of the lower castes should touch the feet of Brahmin boys. Such teachings and traditions horrified the educated Nehru. He would fly into a rage when people tried to touch his feet in a traditional gesture of respect.

Founders of modern India, such as Gandhi and Nehru, wanted modern India to be defined by Christ's teaching. Jesus taught his disciples, "The rulers of the Gentiles lord it over them, and their high officials exercise authority over them. Not so with you. Instead, whoever wants to be great among you must be your servant." (Matthew 20:25-26)

Of course, Indians who no longer study the Bible, do not even remember our founders' vision of transforming India into a nation led by servant-leaders. This book is dedicated to the Union of the Evangelical Students of India because servant-leadership has been the norm in that nationwide organisation. Back in the 1970s, it was usual for someone to go to one of the national conferences of the UESI and, even after four days, not know who the President or the General Secretary of the organisation was. My assessment is that the UESI may be India's largest democratic organistion. None of our political parties that swear by "democracy" are democratically organised. The Congress Party used to be, and, is once again trying to become, a people's party.

The Government of "We the People"

Contrary to what our universities teach, the fact is that modern "democracy" has nothing to do with the democratic experiments of ancient Greek city-states. The greatest Greek philosophers, such as Plato and Aristotle, considered democracy to be the worst of all political systems. Plato hated it because it was Athenian democracy that killed his mentor Socrates.

Plato believed that the ideal Republic should be governed by philosopher-kings. His disciple, Aristotle, trained Alexander the Great to become a philosopher-king. Alexander, however, became one of history's most ruthless tyrants. Imperialism was the only political idea that Greece ever exported to the world.

What we call "democracy" today was born in Scotland, not Athens. Protestant reformers such as John Knox and Andrew Melville understood from the Bible that the Lord Jesus died to purchase Satan's slaves to make them sons of God. As Revelation 5: 9-10 says,

"You were slain,

And have redeemed us to God by Your blood...

And have made us kings and priests to our God;

And we shall reign on the earth." (New King James Bible)

Sonship is kingship if your father is the King. Scottish theologian George Buchanan (1506–1582) called it "Popular sovereignty." Later, the idea was summed up in the Latin phrase, "*Vox Populi, vox Dei*." It meant that not the voice of the pope or emperor, but the voice of the people, is the voice of God.

Mahatma Gandhi's eldest grandson, Dr. Kanubhai Gandhi, spent ten days with some of us studying Jesus' Sermon on the Mount (Matthew 5-7). He told us that his grandfather asked him to memorise the Sermon on the Mount because it is the essence of Christ's teaching about the Kingdom of God. Satan's beastly, brutal, and exploitative kingdom is for the powerful. God's Kingdom is for the poor in spirit, the downtrodden, the hungry, the meek, and the mournful.

Jesus had compassion on the victims of European imperialism. In Matthew 11:28-30, he invited them to take up his yoke upon their shoulders:

"Come to me, all you who are weary and burdened, and I will give you rest. Take my yoke upon you and learn from me, for I am gentle and humble in heart, and you will find rest for your souls. For my yoke is easy and my burden is light."

What is the Messiah's "yoke?" Christ's audience knew the answer—the burden of governance. Seven hundred years before the Messiah was born, the prophet Isaiah had prophesied,

"For to us a child is born, to us a son is given,
and the government will be on his shoulders.

And he will be called Wonderful Counselor, Mighty God, Everlasting Father, Prince of Peace.

Of the greatness of his government and peace there will be no end.

He will reign on David's throne and over his kingdom,
establishing and upholding it with justice and righteousness
from that time on and forever.

The zeal of the LORD Almighty will accomplish this. (Isaiah 9: 6-7)

In the Bible, the "Kingdom of God" means that God has given all authority in heaven and on earth to His Son, the Messiah. He is the King of kings, the Lord of lords. The burden, or the "yoke," of governance is upon his shoulders. He invites the victims of Satan's kingdoms—the weary and the heavy-laden—to take the other side of his yoke upon their shoulders. If they want God's Kingdom on earth, then they have to know God and his will. They have to walk with him and take the responsibility to do his will on earth. That is "Popular Sovereignty." The reformers realised that the voice of the people cannot be the voice of God unless the people study and internalise God's word. That was why the reformers promoted universal education.

Democracy will necessarily degenerate if people do not even know God's will. In that case, they can only pursue their self-interest or the interest of their caste, class, or community. Divorcing political independence from God's word is driving Indians back into the slavery of unprincipled and brutal rulers.

John Knox and other reformers did not call their experiment "democracy." They insisted that they were building God's kingdom, or the New Jerusalem. A century later, everyone could see that the Scottish Church and nation were good, but far from perfect. It became embarrassing to call Scotland the New Jerusalem or God's kingdom. That was when the Scottish Enlightenment decided to rename the Scottish experiment more modestly, "Democracy." Nevertheless, until the beginning of the 20th century, most educated people in Protestant nations were familiar with the concept of popular sovereignty. Ideas such as "the voice of the people is the voice of God," and "government of the people, for the people, and by the people," in which citizens take the responsibility (yoke) of governance upon their shoulders, were concepts that had come from the Bible. It was only after 1910 that American universities invented and began to teach the myth that modern democracy came from Greece. Historian David Gress has exposed that myth in his book, *From Plato to NATO*.

The truth is that even at the level of small city-states, democracy never worked in Greece. It has not worked in any of our neighbouring countries, and it has become a sham in India. The only way to prepare "We the people" for responsible, popular sovereignty is to re-educate the nation in God's truth, revealed in his word. To that controversial subject, therefore, we should now turn.

Chapter 10

The Bible and India's Future

India can become one of the world's greatest nations by repenting of her sins and embracing truth.

Regrettably, a segment of the Indian Church has internalised the prevailing culture of corruption. Nevertheless, it is heartening to note that the transformative power of the Bible continues to renew our souls. A new, post-colonial Church is emerging, particularly among the marginalised poor. This Church is being refined through the trials of persecution and holds the potential to catalyse profound reform within the nation.

To illustrate this possibility of transforming India into a truly great nation, I will share an account from the very bottom of our social structure. While the top ten percent of Indians continue to thrive, some scholars contend that the bottom ninety percent of the population endures levels of poverty comparable to, or even worse than, those found in Sub-Saharan Africa.

In 2015, one of my students in Allahabad (now Prayagraj) invited me to visit the slum directly across from my home, on the other side of the Yamuna River. The University forbade us from swimming across, so we made our way on bicycles over the old, colonial-era bridge that seemed to creak under the weight of history.

On the other side, in the heart of the slum, we found a young man, no more than 17 or 18 years old, standing before a group of about thirty children, teaching them. There, amidst the rubble and dust, at the dead end of a street, a classroom of sorts was in progress.

Around us, the air was thick with the rhythm of daily survival. Mothers and sisters washed dishes and cooked over open flames. I could only assume that these families had no indoor kitchens. A few women balanced heavy clay pots on their heads, trudging down to a public tap at the bottom of the slum to fetch water.

The two of us also sat down on the street, at the back of the class. At the end of the session, the students—all Hindu—stood up to sing a Christian song to honour the visiting "Professor." Like their parents, I was also impressed by this volunteer teacher. Let's call him "KD."

I invited KD for dinner on Saturday. After dinner, KD and I strolled around the university campus. He had no bicycle to return to his room. So he spent the night in my home. In the morning, KD attended our church, Yeshu Darbar (The Royal Court of Jesus). That's when I discovered that two years earlier, he had attended a Bible school run by Yeshu Darbar. That's where he learned the Christian songs that he taught in the slum.

KD enjoyed the hospitality and started coming every weekend. Once we became friends, he confided, "Sir, this year, I won't pass my Intermediate (12th grade) exams."

"Why?"

"Because I don't understand maths."

"Why not?"

"Some students understand the teacher. They take private tuition from him. But as a government employee, he's not allowed to run a coaching school. So, his sister-in-law runs the classes and collects the fees on his behalf. He is the real teacher. But I can't afford to pay for the 'tuition.'"

KD's voice carried the weight of an unspoken frustration as he continued. His home was over 100 kilometers away, and his father had sent him to the city to study because he had lost faith in the government-run village school.

"Why doesn't your father believe in education?" I asked.

"He does," KD replied, "But he doesn't think that government schools are of any use, especially in the villages."

"Do you think teachers would do better if they were paid more?" I pressed.

"A teacher earns much more than a farmer does. That's why thousands of people apply for every teaching post. But money can't motivate them to serve us. Some of these teachers don't even want to educate us. They come from higher castes, and they believe knowledge should be reserved for their own kind. We're allowed to sit in their classrooms only because it's the law. They think the power of knowledge should not be shared with lower castes, and in their eyes, we're not even worthy of it."

There it was, the stark injustice laid bare: a system that not only failed to serve but actively denied.

"Why do *you* spend your evenings educating slum children? Do they pay you?" I asked.

"No. No one pays me anything. I walk about two miles to get there."

"So, why do you serve these kids?"

"I am poor because my caste was never given the chance to be educated," KD said. "But I was amazed when I read in the Bible that God loves everyone, no matter where they come from. Even though our teachers often withhold knowledge from us, I believe that God wants to fill the earth with wisdom and understanding. He pours His Spirit of Truth into the hearts of His children, and that gives me hope."

A quiet determination filled his words as he continued, "The greatest reward I receive from my service is the love of the families and the listening ears of the children. They listen to me. I love God and want to fulfill His will on this earth. These children may not go to school, but they absolutely love to learn."

"Don't you live in that slum?" I asked

"No, I live in the city, sharing a small room with four older boys. They're all from my caste, and none of them finished school. They work as casual labourers whenever they can find work. The TV is always on—

24 hours a day—and it makes it impossible for me to study. The board exams are only three months away, and I'm terrified I'll fail. But my roommates don't seem to care. They don't think studying will change anything. In their eyes, it's inevitable—eventually, I'll end up just like them, doing whatever work I can find, struggling day by day."

"No!" I said emphatically. "You are India's most valuable hope. Your father is wise. You should study, and you should continue to teach those kids in the slum. Please move into my home for the next three months. I'll help you prepare for your exams."

The university had given me a desktop computer that I wasn't using. So, I set it up for KD and enrolled him on Khan Academy to study math. He read English but didn't understand it. I taught him to use Google Translate and Dictionary.com to understand online lessons. I also gave him a bilingual Hindi-English Bible to enhance his learning of English.

Our meal times became his English class, with plenty of detours to discuss the Bible, theology, philosophy, history, religion, sociology, current affairs, and science. KD fell in love with Mathematics.

After exams, he had to wait for three months for the results. So, he asked if he could start a new class in another slum and prepare for admission to the university.

A while back, our university purchased a few bicycles for the Vice Chancellor and his security team. Later, it prohibited him from cycling to work. I asked the registrar if KD could use one of those bicycles to start a class for slum children. The registrar was pleased to help.

A widow invited KD to teach the kids under a tree in front of her home. She had three little children but couldn't look after them, as she spent the whole day collecting plastic bottles. She had to feed her family, including a brother who was dying of tuberculosis.

KD agreed, and I bought him a large mat to cover the mud floor. Five days a week, he taught a group of 20 to 30 children, ranging in age from 4 to 15. Once a week, I teamed up with him for a session where we played with the children, and I answered their questions about general knowledge.

That summer, Dheeraj came to visit me. He works in the IT industry in Texas, USA. KD's class so impressed him that he decided to donate some tablets. These would allow the students to sit in small groups and study lessons appropriate for their age. KD wouldn't need to teach the same lesson to a diverse age group. He could just walk around to make sure that the students were sharing the tablets and helping each other study.

Dheeraj purchased 13 tablets directly from an Indian manufacturer at a significant discount. KD traveled to Pune to collect them and took the time to learn how to use them. The slum had neither electricity nor internet access, so we preloaded the tablets with the state-approved curricula for grades 1 through 10. Each evening, KD would bring the tablets to my home to recharge them, ensuring they were ready for the next day's lessons.

This was a revolution: all of a sudden, the slum kids had entered the digital age! When I started school, we had to learn how to use slate and chalk, paper and pencil. These undernourished children from poor homes were being prepared for the Information Age.

Soon after Dheeraj, another dear friend, Rebecca Shourie, sent me a huge jar of delicious fish pickle. We don't make that in North India. She did because she was born in Kerala, South India. She had devoted her life to building and running a school in Madhya Pradesh.

KD had never eaten fish pickle. He loved it so much that he announced that he would learn how to make it. Then he could eat it every day, with every meal! I suggested that instead of making it himself, he should encourage the slum women to learn how to make fish pickle. He could package their produce and sell it to the 1200 staff members of the university. This would enable him to eat and also make some money.

When they were informed about this, the possibility of doing something better than collecting garbage excited the slum mothers. The proposal was perfect because they lived on the bank of the Yamuna, just below the fresh fish market.

There was a little problem: none of them had a kitchen. A lady staff member at the university offered to teach the illiterate ladies how to make fish pickle in her kitchen. I lent KD Rs. 200 to buy fish, oil, and spices. After selling some of the pickles, he returned my loan. The women were so enthused that it took no time for three or four of them to master the new skill.

"We have no kitchen! Where can we practice this art and earn a living?" they asked. I suggested that they could use my kitchen when I was in my office. Then, together, we could explore the possibility of renting a room near their slum.

When they first came to use my kitchen, I made chai for them and invited them to sit at the dining table for some simple snacks. They hesitated, unsure if I knew what I was doing. They were "untouchable," therefore, no one had ever invited them to sit and eat at the dining table in their home.

As they shared about their families and children, I inquired if anyone objects to a Christian teaching their children. One of them replied,

"Yes, one day a group of angry young men came and asked who KD was and what he was teaching our kids."

"How did you answer?"

"I told them that he comes from the university across the river."

"Does the university pay him?"

"No. He is waiting for his Board results so that he can study there."

"Does he ask you to become Christian?"

"Once he took our children to sing in Yeshu Darbar. But no one has asked them to convert."

"Why do you allow your children to learn about a foreign god?"

"I got irritated and asked them, 'Why don't you teach our children? Why don't you invite them to become priests in your temple?'"

The ladies agreed that a long-term solution to their need would be to rent a community center with a kitchen and storage. If it had more rooms, they could bring their children along to study. On Sundays, it could be used for Satsang (worship service).

One mother added that since they come from different castes, spiritual nurture may help the families to cooperate. Unity would overcome caste and class prejudices. Another mother endorsed the idea: "No cooperative would work without cultivating trustworthy character in members and leaders."

The first giggled, "We definitely need someone to teach our men to invest in their children. We live in slums because they drink and gamble. If they come here, they may learn to make tea for their families."

"Yes," said the other. "They bathe in the holy river, but their bad habits are never washed away. They talk about Dr. Ambedkar and blame Caste for all our problems. But half of our troubles will be over if our husbands change."

The ladies understood that renting a multi-purpose community center would be viable only if it is used full time to make other pickles such as mango, lemon, chilli, garlic, ginger, carrot, and cauliflower. Such produce will need to be branded and sold in the market... as long as people do not know that low-caste women made them.

Some of the ladies could learn to make sweets and fancy snacks, while others could use that kitchen for simpler products such as roasted, fried, or boiled peanuts. All these things could be sold under the same brand name.

One of them exclaimed that she wouldn't need to bathe in the river. She could shower in the center!

The practical difficulty was obvious: only the wealthy, "upper" caste families had houses to rent. Why would they rent a house to a group of illiterate, poorly dressed, low-caste women who had no jobs or regular income?

"What," I asked, "if someone organised you as a cooperative and negotiated a rent agreement on your behalf?"

That might work, they thought.

A cooperative would open up the possibility of government grants and bank loans. Some kind doctor or nurse might be willing to use a part of the space for a weekly clinic for us. But we will need someone educated to organise the cooperative to get the ball rolling. We couldn't pay them upfront. They will need to take their commission after the cooperative begins to make money.

"Yes!" remarked one lady thoughtfully. "The organiser will have to work like a farmer who ploughs his field, borrows seed, irrigates, and protects his crop until the harvest. Only then does he return the loans and make some money."

"Where will we find such a social farmer?" mused a mother. "Our *netas* (petty politicians) blame others and ask for our votes. Even our husbands don't care for us or our children."

"Well," answered another, "Don't we have KD caring for us and the Sir supporting him?" The lady pointed towards me.

I was embarrassed. I responded by pointing to a cross: "I'm only following Jesus Christ, who shed his own blood on a cross to give us abundant life. He was a different guru. He taught that a good shepherd leaves his ninety-nine sheep to find and rescue the one who is lost. He didn't ask for alms and donations because he taught that it was more blessed to give than to receive."

The discussions continued, flowing back and forth for a few days, full of energy and ideas. In the midst of it all, KD's results were released—he had passed the Board exams with First Division honours! The monsoon arrived just as he received his admission to our university. The heavy rains made it impossible to hold classes outdoors, under a tree

The abrupt ending, coming so soon after such a promising start, made it clear to us that a program like this requires more than just good intentions—it needs a church with stable leadership and committed volunteers. A church dedicated to educating children and transforming communities must be led by evangelists and pastors who are true shepherds, not merely hirelings seeking a paycheck.

This is not wishful thinking. Kerala is India's most educated state with a literacy rate of over 96%. In their language, Malayalam, the word for "school" is *Pallikudam*. That means the building next to the Church. As early as the 19th century, Kerala embraced the European idea of "Parish school." The church, not the state, spread literacy in Western Europe, North America, and Kerala.

Likewise, Mizoram, India's most Christian state is the second most literate state. It is close to 92% literate. KD's experiment demonstrates that the Bible can do for all of India what it did in Western Europe, Kerala and Mizoram. In fact, technology allows us to do better. Now, with help from the internet, every church can offer college and university-level courses.

KD helped some of the boys get admission into government schools. But what about the girls? I had been visiting the slum once a week, but I had not paid attention to the fact that no girl over the age of 12 was attending the class.

"Where are your older sisters?" I asked the kids.

"Oh, they got married."

"Do they visit you after marriage?"

"Not really; they live far away," was the hesitant response.

A little probing opened my eyes to a grim reality: in many cases, pimps arrive in the slums with cars laden with sweets, clothes, and jewelry. They bring alcohol for the fathers and neighbours, pay a previously agreed-upon price, and take the girls as their "brides." Mothers, fearing incest and unable to shield their daughters from inevitable pregnancies, reluctantly agree to sell them.

Properly arranged marriages are a distant dream, requiring matching castes, horoscopes, and dowries. Even these marriages often send girls back to villages with no real prospects for earning a living. Boys from their caste who work in the city demand educated brides and hefty dowries, leaving these girls with no way out.

Poverty is powerlessness, a relentless tide of helplessness. Yet, amidst this darkness, could sex traffickers' manipulative "love" be countered by the genuine love of churches and shepherds—enough to give these girls a chance at a future?

Could the digital curricula envisioned for proposed educational co-operatives include practical courses in shopping, cooking, decorating, serving, hospitality, pedicure, manicure, massage, geriatric care, and prenatal and postnatal care for mothers and infants? To ensure hands-on training and valuable experience, students could be placed as interns with local businesses, physicians, clinics, and hospitals.

Advanced topics, particularly in STEM disciplines (Science, Technology, Engineering, and Mathematics), would benefit from leveraging 3D Virtual Reality technologies. With devices like phones, tablets, and computers already revolutionising language instruction, some girls could be trained to become bi-vocational missionary nurses, serving in regions such as China, Japan, South Korea, the Middle East, and even the West.

Training Nation-Builders

Clearly, our culture is not producing leaders like KD. According to data collected by UDISE+ (Unified District Information System for Education Plus) during 2021–22, India had over 9.5 million teachers. How many of these "trained" teachers believed, as KD did, that the true wealth of the nation lies buried in the hearts and minds of its people? That educating the next generation means bringing out the national wealth?

KD's father didn't think that teachers were doing what they were paid to do. His father must have transmitted that perspective to KD, but at a conscious level, KD was inspired by the Bible, which taught,

"Blessed are those who find wisdom,
those who gain understanding,
for she is more profitable than silver
and yields better returns than gold.
She is more precious than rubies;
nothing you desire can compare with her.
Long life is in her right hand;
in her left hand are riches and honour.
Her ways are pleasant ways,
and all her paths are peace.
She is a tree of life to those who take hold of her;
those who hold her fast will be blessed." (Proverbs 3:13–18)

For thousands of years, Hindu society has prohibited lower castes from pursuing knowledge and wisdom. The nation has been the loser.

Wealth, far more precious than gold or petroleum, remains buried. It was not brought out, refined, and used to bless the world.

I supported KD because he sought to liberate a people bound by the chains of false spirituality. KD's Mathematics teacher was deeply knowledgeable and skilled in his craft, but he lacked God's vision for humanity, education, and national transformation. Through His Word, God reveals His vision. While the teacher excelled as a professional, KD was a shepherd who lovingly cared for the sheep. KD caught hold of God's vision.

India can change if we fill it with the vision, wisdom and knowledge of God. A first step will be to acquire/create the world's best KG-12 curricula and make it available to everyone for free.

Artificial Intelligence will need to be used to contextualise some courses. Assam's history is different from Andhra's. Courses on agriculture may vary, but Algebra and AI can remain the same.

Online school curricula will be used by Shepherd-Teachers who mentor students. I call them *Academic Pastors*. This diploma and university-level training will have options. An Academic Pastor, mentoring preschool children will have different training than someone preparing to mentor intermediate (senior High School) or College students.

All aspiring teachers should study the book that created modern India and the modern world, that is, the Bible. It is the only effective antidote to corruption because it cultivates the fear of God as no other book does: "The fear of the Lord is the beginning of knowledge, but fools despise wisdom and instruction." (Proverbs 1:7). Only the Bible has ever given to India a morally trustworthy "Steel Frame" of civil, police, and judicial services.

India's moral degeneration (and also the West's) is the consequence of removing the Bible as education's foundation. Recently, news media in the USA and social media in India are reporting that Apple Inc has asked 185 of its well-educated and well-paid staff to resign. Many of them are highly educated, very qualified Indians.

Why?

The IRS uncovered a scam involving 185 Apple employees who

abused the company's charity matching program. The policy was simple: if an employee donated $10,000 to a nonprofit (501(c)(3)) organisation and submitted the receipt, Apple would match the donation by giving the same amount to the same charity.

These employees donated, got Apple to match the donation, claimed the tax deduction, and then secretly took their original donation back from the charity. In the end, the charity only received $10,000, while the employees pocketed $10,000 in untaxed money.

Now, Apple will lose its highly skilled, experienced and competent staff, purely because they were willfully corrupt and dishonest. The IRS is likely to investigate similar frauds in other multinational companies.

The Lesson: The West is awakening to the rude reality of corruption. Cultures are not equal. Indian Institutes of Technology and institutions of Higher Education can teach STEM and produce skillful graduates. But reliable, God-fearing character is produced by the word of God, not by high-profile universities and labs.

It is crucial to note that the Bible is far more than a book about ethics—it is a transformative force that has shaped modern thought and society. In my book, *The Bible and the Making of Modern India*, I have drawn attention to the following facts:

1. The idea that the human mind can and should know the truth comes from the Bible. No Hindu ashram ever grew to become a university, because Hinduism does not believe that the intellect can know truth. As Acharya (Osho) Rajneesh taught, yoga, mantras, and meditations as techniques to suppress and kill the intellect.

2. The modern belief, that human beings can understand the world and establish their dominion over it through science and technology, comes from the Bible.

3. It is only the Bible that uniquely affirms the sanctity of marriage, defining it as a lifelong, exclusive union between a man and a woman for mutual care, the raising of children, and the nurturing of families.

4. As forthcoming volumes in this series will explain in greater detail, modern ideas of nation—including, national sovereignty, the rule of law, the Indian Penal Code, constitutional governance, the rights and

sovereignty of citizens, etc.—are deeply rooted in Biblical principles

5. The Bible alone provides the philosophical foundation for believing that human beings have equal value, dignity, liberty, and rights

6. The Bible makes progress possible by teaching that human choices are valuable, have meaning, and shape our future for better or for worse.

While each Academic Pastor will develop professional expertise in one or more subjects of his/her choice, each of them will learn to be a shepherd who nurtures the sheep. I didn't teach Math to KD. He learnt it himself. I just shepherded him as he was shepherding the children and youths in the slum.

Academic Pastors, supported by a great online curriculum and mentoring students face-to-face, will turn every church into a center of high-quality intellectual, moral, and vocational education. Millions of churches promoting and nurturing educational cooperatives will build lives. They will make education a ministry of the church in discipling nations.

How Shall We Do It?

In partnership with the worldwide body of Christ, The Third Education Revolution movement will create a new online Truthpedia-cum-university. Utilising AI, Truthpedia will give away personalised, contextualised High School curricula for free in many languages. That will make it possible for the poorest church to start an educational cooperative. This will be the starting point for economic and medical cooperatives.

Charging a small fee for college courses will pay for the entire operation. Truthpedia will partner with existing, accredited universities to offer degrees. It will seek accreditation for its own university as it develops a new system of offering credit points for everything a student reads, hears, watches, or studies. Truthpedia will mimic what airlines do – recording and crediting every mile that a member flies. Likewise, when a student reads an article in Truthpedia or watches a video or a movie, Truthpedia will credit him/her points. If they take a test on that subject, they will get extra points. This will enable a future employer to know what an applicant has studied.

Along with Teacher's Training, Truthpedia will also create a special, university level course on Nation Building. This will be a modular program, allowing students to choose different modules each month or quarter. Students will be able to study disciplines such as history, law, economics, politics, business, leadership, administration, philosophy, science, technology, pre-med, pre-engineering, sociology, religion, ethics, literature, culture, international relations, music, fine arts, general knowledge, journalism, writing, and debating skills.

Each module will have internship and practical experience options. These courses will prepare students for a spectrum of competitive exams, including civil services, and also for entry into professional, vocational courses. As a result, some students will be equipped to start their own businesses or service projects.

These paid courses will also generate the financial resources needed to develop other university level courses. Truthpedia will go beyond academic subjects to make it possible for a student to study a topic in detail and participate in research. Truthpedia will also serve as a knowledge bank which encourages experts to debate ideas. It will supplement the details of what cannot be covered in limited modules.

A Unifying Worldview

The Bible is God's perspective on creation and man's place on the earth. Therefore, it will serve as the worldview foundation for the knowledge bank for all academic disciplines and all of life. As the Psalmist put it, "The unfolding of your words gives light; it gives understanding to the simple." (Psalm 119:130). And, "I gain understanding from your precepts; therefore, I hate every wrong path. Your word is a lamp for my feet, a light on my path." (Psalm 119:104-105).

Incidentally, this vision is not new. The university movement, including in India, owes its existence to the Bible. Theology was the Queen of all sciences because in Jesus are hidden all the treasures of wisdom and knowledge. (Colossians 2:3).

C. S. Lewis pointed this out to Oxford's Socratic Club in 1944.

Speaking on the topic, "Is Theology Poetry" (meaning: is theology imagination or fiction?) Lewis said, "I believe in Christianity as I believe that the sun has risen—not only because I see it, but because by it I see everything else."

Oxford's motto is "Dominus Illuminatio Mea" (The Lord is my light). It comes from Psalm 27:1. Lewis' point was that by rejecting God's light, every faculty has become an Academic silo—a source of darkness, disconnected from life. By rejecting divine revelation, philosophy has been forced to give up the hope that the human mind can know the truth. The contemporary "hermeneutic of suspicion" has begun to look at every statement as someone's attempt to manipulate and control others. That is why our post-truth world sees the best of investigative journalism as "Fake News."

Many human ideas deceive and enslave, yet India's national motto, *Satya Mev Jayate*—Truth Alone Triumphs—reminds us that truth liberates. It is God's Word, the ultimate truth, that freed India and must remain the cornerstone of our future.

Study Guide

By George Anthony Paul

Chapter 1: The Bible and the Idea of India

Discussion and Study Questions

Understanding the Chapter

- What historical evidence does Mangalwadi present to show that India lacked a unified identity before British rule? (p. 1, para. 2–4)
- How does Mangalwadi trace the origins of the name "India" to the Bible? (p. 5, para. 5–6)
- What role did British missionaries play in changing caste and tribe consciousness into a national consciousness? (p. 6, para. 3)
- How did biblical teachings challenge India's Caste and power-based governance? (p. 9, para. 2–4)
- How did the Mughal empire differ from the biblical model of governance? (p. 3, para. 1)

Analysing the Argument

- What are the key premises of Mangalwadi's argument, and what evidence does he provide for each? (Refer to the Argument Structure section)
- How does Mangalwadi differentiate biblical nationalism from traditional Hindu governance? (p. 7, para. 1–3)
- Does the author provide sufficient evidence to support his claim that the Bible was instrumental in shaping modern India? Why or why not?
- What was William Carey's role in introducing literacy and social reform in India? (p. 8, para. 1–3)

Critical Thinking & Further Discussion

- What counter arguments might be presented against Mangalwadi's thesis?
- What other factors besides biblical influence contributed to India's national identity?
- How does the author's perspective challenge mainstream historical narratives about India's formation?
- How do the Westminster model and biblical principles align with India's constitutional framework? (p. 10, para. 1–3)
- In what ways does renaming India challenge the biblical historical framework? (p. 11, para. 3)

Summary

Chapter 1, The Bible and the Idea of India, challenges the notion that India's national identity is indigenous. Vishal Mangalwadi argues that the modern concept of India as a unified nation-state is largely a product of biblical influence introduced through European explorers, British colonial governance, and missionary education. He asserts that pre-colonial India lacked a singular national identity, functioning instead as a fragmented collection of kingdoms, castes, and religious communities.

The chapter traces the origins of the name "India" to biblical references, which were adopted by European explorers and later by British rulers. Mangalwadi contends that biblical ideas of governance, justice, equality, and nationhood played a crucial role in shaping India's modern institutions. Unlike the traditional caste-based and regional governance of Hinduism and the hierarchical structure of the Mughal Empire, the Bible provided a vision of unity that emphasised equal human dignity and national sovereignty. Missionaries such as William Carey helped shape India's intellectual and legal framework by promoting education, linguistic development, and social reform.

Mangalwadi's argument suggests that India's transition into a democratic nation with a constitutional government is largely a result of biblical principles, rather than a natural evolution of Hindu or Mughal traditions. The chapter also critiques the current movement to rename India and erase its biblical roots, arguing that such efforts ignore the fundamental role the Bible played in forming modern India.

Argument Structure: Premises, Evidence, and Conclusion

Premise 1: Pre-Colonial India Lacked a Unified National Identity

Evidence:

- Historically, India was divided into multiple kingdoms, tribes, and caste-based communities (p. 1, para. 2–4).
- Hinduism, unlike Christianity or Islam, did not provide a centralised religious or legal system to unify diverse groups (p. 2, para. 3).
- Mughal rule was focused on imperial expansion rather than the development of a national consciousness (p. 3, para. 1).
- Example: The caste system's rigidity prevented the development of a shared national identity (p. 4, para. 2).

Premise 2: The Name "India" and the Concept of Nationhood Were Introduced Through Biblical Influences

Evidence:

- The Latin Bible translated the Persian term "Hind" into "India," influencing European explorers like Vasco da Gama and Columbus (p. 5, para. 5–6).
- British administrators and missionaries adopted this biblical reference, reinforcing the idea of a united India (p. 6, para. 3).
- Before British rule, there was no widely accepted indigenous name for a political entity encompassing the entire subcontinent (p. 6, para. 5).

Premise 3: Biblical Principles Provided the Foundation for Modern Governance in India

Evidence:

- British missionaries, beginning with William Carey, introduced universal education, literacy, and legal reforms based on biblical principles (p. 8, para. 1–3).
- The British legal and administrative systems emphasised justice, equality, and individual rights, concepts that were largely absent from pre-colonial Indian governance (p. 9, para. 2–4).
- The Westminster model of governance, which India adopted, was deeply rooted in biblical teachings on self-governance and moral responsibility (p. 10, para. 1).

Conclusion:

India's modern national identity, democratic governance, and legal systems owe much to biblical influence rather than to an organic evolution of indigenous traditions. The Bible's emphasis on human dignity, justice, and national unity provided the intellectual and moral foundation for the formation of a modern India. This challenges the narrative that India's progress was solely a result of its Hindu or Mughal past (p. 11, para. 3).

Key Themes & Ideas

- **Lack of an Indigenous National Identity (p. 1, para. 2–4)**

India's pre-colonial political landscape was fragmented, lacking a unifying national vision.

Hinduism's caste-based structure prevented the development of a common national consciousness.

- **Biblical Origins of the Name "India" and Nationalism (p. 5, para. 4–5)**

The name "India" emerged from biblical references and was later reinforced by European explorers and British colonial rulers.

The Bible introduced the idea of a nation as a self-governing entity under a common moral and legal code.

- **Contrasts Between Biblical and Hindu Governance Models (p. 7, para. 1–3)**

Hinduism supported a hierarchical, caste-based system, whereas the Bible emphasised justice, human equality, and moral responsibility. Mughal rule was centralised but lacked a national framework beyond imperial expansion.

- **Role of Missionaries and Reformers (p. 8, para. 1–3)**

Christian missionaries contributed to the development of vernacular education, the press, and legal systems based on biblical principles. Their work laid the groundwork for modern democratic governance in India.

Chapter 2 – The Bible and India's Renaissance

Discussion and Study Questions

Understanding the Chapter

- What role did oral traditions play in ancient Indian culture, and why did Sanskrit fail to become India's common language? (p. 13, para. 2-4)
- How did the lack of written records affect historical documentation in India? (p. 14, para. 2-3)
- What were the contributions of James Prinsep in deciphering ancient Indian scripts, and why was this significant? (p. 13, para. 4)
- What evidence suggests that Jews arrived in India after the Babylonian exile? (p. 14, para. 4 – p. 15, para. 1)
- How does the author describe the early influence of Christianity in India? (p. 15, para. 2-4)

Analysing the Argument

- How does Mangalwadi argue that the Bible played a foundational role in India's Renaissance? What historical evidence does he provide? (p. 16, para. 2-5)

- How did biblical principles influence India's transition from a caste-based society to a more inclusive nation? (p. 18, para. 1-3)
- What are the key ways that biblical teachings challenged India's traditional view of governance and law? (p. 19, para. 2-4)
- How does Mangalwadi contrast biblical ethics with Hindu social hierarchies? (p. 20, para. 1-3)
- Why does the author believe the Bible was instrumental in shaping India's modern intellectual landscape? (p. 21, para. 2-4)

Critical Thinking & Further Discussion

- What are some counterarguments to Mangalwadi's assertion that the Bible was central to India's intellectual and social development?
- Could India's Renaissance have happened without biblical influence? What alternative factors might have played a role?
- How does Mangalwadi's perspective challenge mainstream historical narratives about India's modernisation?
- In what ways did the Bible inspire reforms in education, law, and social justice in India? (p. 22, para. 2-4)
- How do contemporary scholars interpret the influence of Christianity on India's history compared to Mangalwadi's argument?

Summary

Chapter 2, The Bible and India's Renaissance, explores how biblical principles influenced India's cultural, intellectual, and moral transformation. Mangalwadi argues that India's Renaissance was significantly shaped by the Bible-inspired missionaries and civil servants rather than being an organic evolution of Hindu, Buddhist or Islamic traditions.

The chapter discusses the nature of ancient Indian civilization, emphasising its reliance on oral traditions rather than written historical records. While Buddhist scholars developed written texts, the Vedas—the core of Hindu sacred literature—remained unwritten for centuries. The lack of a written script for Sanskrit further complicated historical preservation and national unity. British scholars like James Prinsep and archeologists played a crucial role in deciphering ancient scripts, providing insight into India's lost past.

Mangalwadi presents historical accounts suggesting that Jewish communities arrived in India after the Babylonian exile, receiving royal patronage to settle in Kerala. Christianity's early presence in India, particularly through the Apostle Thomas, further set the stage for later transformations.

The core argument of the chapter is that biblical teachings provided a foundation for India's intellectual and social development. Biblical ethics challenged the caste system, promoted literacy, and introduced legal and governance models that emphasised equality and human dignity. The Bible's influence extended to education, as missionaries translated texts and created linguistic tools that revolutionised literacy in India.

Mangalwadi contends that India's modernisation and national unity were not purely indigenous developments but were significantly influenced by Christian thought, including its Secular Humanist version that denied some key biblical doctrines. He critiques the idea that Hindu or Mughal traditions were responsible for India's progress, arguing that these systems often reinforced social divisions and authoritarian rule. Instead, biblical teachings inspired reforms in law, education, governance, and social justice.

Argument Structure: Premises, Evidence, and Conclusion

Premise 1: Ancient India Lacked a Unified Written Tradition

Evidence

- The Vedas, Hinduism's most sacred texts, were unwritten for centuries (p. 13, para. 2-4).
- Sanskrit had no native script, limiting its ability to unify India linguistically (p. 14, para. 1).
- British Indologist James Prinsep deciphered the Ashoka Pillar inscriptions, revealing historical insights previously lost (p. 13, para. 4).

- Oral traditions often transformed historical facts into myths, making them difficult to verify (p. 14, para. 2-3).

Premise 2: Biblical Influence Played a Central Role in India's Intellectual Awakening

Evidence:

- Jewish communities settled in India as early as 562 BC, establishing trade and religious centers (p. 14, para. 4 – p. 15, para. 1).
- St. Thomas, one of Christ's apostles, is believed to have brought Christianity to India in the first century (p. 15, para. 2-3).
- The Bible's moral and ethical teachings challenged the rigid social structures of Hinduism, particularly the caste system (p. 18, para. 2-4).
- Christian missionaries introduced literacy and education to marginalised communities (p. 19, para. 1-3).

Premise 3: Biblical Principles Inspired India's Modern Reforms

Evidence:

- Christian missionaries pioneered India's first printing presses, democratising access to knowledge (p. 21, para. 1-2).
- Biblical principles promoted the idea of human dignity and equality, influencing social reformers like Raja Ram Mohan Roy (p. 22, para. 2-3).
- Biblical teachings on justice and morality laid the foundation for India's legal and political institutions (p. 23, para. 1-2).

Conclusion

Mangalwadi argues that the Bible was a catalyst for India's intellectual, legal, and social transformation. Without biblical influence, India's caste or tribe-based social hierarchy and fatalistic worldview might have persisted unchallenged. The chapter suggests that India's modern identity owes much to the ethical and intellectual revolution sparked by biblical teachings, challenging the dominant narrative that credits India's Renaissance solely to indigenous traditions.

Key Themes & Ideas

- **Oral vs. Written Tradition:**

The absence of a written script for Sanskrit and the reliance on oral myths contributed to historical distortions.

- **Christianity's Early Influence in India:**

Evidence of Jewish and Christian settlements predating British colonialism.

- **The Role of Christian Missionaries:**

Contributions to literacy, education, linguistic and intellectual development.

- **Biblical Ethics vs. Hindu Social Hierarchies:**

The Bible's teachings on equality contrasted with the caste system.

- **Legal and Political Reforms:**

The Bible's influence on justice, governance, and constitutionalism in India.

Chapter 3: The Bible Explodes Indian Fatalism

Discussion and Study Questions

- **Understanding the Chapter**
  - How does Mangalwadi describe the fatalistic worldview of pre-modern India? (p. 27, para. 2–4)
  - What evidence does the author provide to show that fatalism hindered social and economic progress in India? (p. 28, para. 1–3)
  - How did the Bible challenge the philosophy of karma and reincarnation? (p. 31, para. 4–6)
  - What was Premchand's critique of Indian fatalism, and how does it

align with biblical teachings on work and progress? (p. 27, para. 3–5)
- How did the Bible's teaching on governance influence British civil servants in India? (p. 29, para. 2–4)
- What role did Charles Grant play in advocating biblical reforms in India? (p. 30, para. 3–5)
- How did missionary education counter the effects of fatalism and promote social reform? (p. 32, para. 1–3)

Analysing the Argument

- What are the key premises of Mangalwadi's argument, and what evidence does he provide for each? (Refer to the Argument Structure section)
- How does Mangalwadi differentiate biblical teachings on justice from Hindu ideas of karma and social hierarchy? (p. 31, para. 3–5)
- Does the author provide sufficient evidence to support his claim that the Bible was instrumental in changing Indian society? Why or why not?
- How did biblical principles influence leaders like Mahatma Gandhi and Dr. B. R. Ambedkar in their opposition to caste-based discrimination? (p. 33, para. 2–4)

Critical Thinking & Further Discussion

- What counter-arguments might be presented against Mangalwadi's thesis?
- Are there other historical or cultural factors besides biblical influence that contributed to India's shift away from fatalism?
- How does Mangalwadi's perspective challenge mainstream historical narratives about India's social transformation?
- In what ways does the author's argument align with or differ from the views of Indian reformers like Raja Ram Mohan Roy and Ishwar Chandra Vidyasagar? (p. 34, para. 1–3)

Summary

Chapter 3, The Bible Explodes Indian Fatalism, explores how biblical teachings transformed India's deeply entrenched fatalistic worldview. Vishal Mangalwadi argues that Indian society, governed by the doctrine of karma and reincarnation, historically accepted suffering as an inescapable consequence of past actions. This belief led to a resignation toward illiteracy, poverty, injustice, and social stagnation.

The chapter illustrates how British missionaries and reformers, inspired by the Bible, actively challenged these ideas. The biblical emphasis on individual dignity, work ethic, and social justice inspired movements for education, governance, and social reforms. Figures like Charles Grant, William Carey, and later Indian reformers like Dr. B. R. Ambedkar drew from biblical principles to advocate for human rights, equality, and economic development.

Mangalwadi highlights how Indian literature, such as the works of Premchand, reflects the transition from fatalistic despair to an aspiration for change. The Bible's portrayal of God as a just and active presence in history—rather than a distant, indifferent deity—offered a compelling alternative to fatalism, fostering a belief in individual and societal progress.

By contrasting biblical teachings with Hindu doctrines that justified social hierarchy, Mangalwadi argues that the Bible played a pivotal role in shaping modern India's intellectual and moral framework.

Argument Structure: Premises, Evidence, and Conclusion

Premise 1: Fatalism Dominated Pre-Modern Indian Thought

Evidence:

- Indian peasants accepted oppression and poverty as part of their destiny (p. 27, para. 2–4).
- The belief in karma discouraged efforts to improve social conditions (p. 28, para. 1–3).
- Premchand's writings vividly depict how fatalism affected everyday life (p. 27, para. 3–5).
- Premise 2: The Bible Introduced a New Work Ethic and Hope for

Progress

Evidence:

- Biblical teachings on human dignity and justice directly opposed the caste system (p. 31, para. 3–5).
- Charles Grant and British evangelicals campaigned against corruption and social oppression (p. 30, para. 3–5).
- Missionary education introduced the idea that individuals could change their circumstances through knowledge and effort (p. 32, para. 1–3).

Premise 3: Biblical Reformers Inspired Social and Political Change

Evidence:

- Dr. B. R. Ambedkar, who led the movement against caste discrimination, was influenced by Christian ideas of equality (p. 33, para. 2–4).
- The introduction of democratic governance was based on biblical principles of justice and moral responsibility (p. 29, para. 2–4).
- The concept of rule of law and human rights that shaped India's Constitution have biblical roots (p. 34, para. 1–3).

Conclusion: The Bible Played a Pivotal Role in Overcoming Fatalism

India's transition from a fatalistic society to one that values progress in respecting individual dignity, education, and development is largely due to biblical influence. The Bible's teachings provided an alternative to the caste-based and karma-driven worldview, inspiring movements for social reform and governance that emphasised equality and human rights.

Key Themes & Ideas

1. The Influence of Fatalism on Indian Society (p. 27, para. 2–4)

- Indian peasants historically accepted oppression as destiny.

- The caste system reinforced a rigid social hierarchy.
- The philosophy of karma discouraged individual or social change.

2. The Bible's Opposition to Fatalism (p. 31, para. 3–5)

- The Bible teaches that humans are created in God's image with freedom and dignity.
- Biblical narratives promote the idea of justice and accountability.
- The Protestant work ethic, introduced by missionaries and Mahatma Gandhi, encouraged progress and reform.

3. Missionary Education and Reform (p. 32, para. 1–3)

- Missionaries established schools that empowered lower-caste children.
- Christian ideas of justice and morality influenced early Indian reformers.
- The Bible introduced the concept of governance based on servant leadership that respects individual rights and responsibility.

4. The Bible's Role in Shaping Indian Political and Legal Systems (p. 34, para. 1–3)

- The Indian Constitution reflects biblical principles of justice and equality.
- Missionary-reformers fought against corruption and caste discrimination.
- Leaders like Ambedkar used biblical principles to frame legal protections for marginalised communities.

Chapter 4: The Bible Reformed the British Raj

1. Discussion and Study Questions

Understanding the Chapter

- What was the state of corruption among British rulers between 1765 and 1820, and how does the author compare it to modern Indian governance? (p. 39)
- How did the Indian Civil Services (ICS) develop under colonial rule, and why did Vallabhbhai Patel refer to it as the "Steel Frame of India"? (p. 39–40)
- What role did the Bible and the Evangelical movement play in reforming British administration in India? (p. 40)
- How did the work of Christian missionaries influence India's civil services and legal framework? (p. 41)
- Why did Peter Drucker describe Indian Civil Services as Britain's "supreme administrative accomplishment," and how was this connected to biblical teachings? (p. 40–41)
- What impact did missionary education have on instilling ethical character in civil servants? (p. 42–43)
- How did British officials trained in Bible-based moral values contribute to governance, and what changes occurred after India gained independence? (p. 43–44)

Analysing the Argument

- What are the key premises of Mangalwadi's argument that the Bible was central to reforming British rule in India? (Refer to the Argument Structure section)
- How does the author contrast British colonial rule before and after the influence of the Bible? (p. 39–40)
- How did the Protestant work ethic influence the behavior of British officials in India? (p. 41–42)
- What role did Charles Grant and William Wilberforce play in transforming the governance of the East India Company? (p. 42–43)
- How does the author evaluate the long-term consequences of biblical influence on Indian governance, and what does he suggest about its decline in post-independence India? (p. 44–45)

Critical Thinking & Further Discussion

- Could the ethical transformation of the British administration have occurred without the influence of the Bible?
- How does the author's perspective challenge mainstream historical narratives about colonialism and governance?
- What counter-arguments could be made against Mangalwadi's claim that biblical principles were the foundation of just governance in India?
- How does the development of governance under British rule compare to governance in other colonial settings?
- What lessons from this chapter can be applied to contemporary issues of corruption and administration in India today?

Summary

Chapter 4, The Bible Reformed the British Raj, examines how the Bible played a crucial role in transforming British colonial governance in India. Vishal Mangalwadi argues that the rule of the British East India Company began as very corrupt but the Evangelical movement and Bible-based education instilled a moral framework that reformed the civil services.

Sardar Vallabhbhai Patel famously described the Indian Civil Services (ICS) as the "Steel Frame of India," recognising its role in maintaining order and justice. The chapter explores how biblical principles of integrity, justice, and service influenced British administrators, many of whom were sons of pastors trained in the Bible. Figures like Charles Grant and William Wilberforce led the movement to reform the East India Company, advocating ethical governance.

Mangalwadi highlights that missionary education promoted character development alongside intellectual training, resulting in ethical administrators. He contrasts this with the post-independence decline in ethical governance, arguing that modern Indian bureaucracy suffers from corruption due to the removal of biblical values from education and public service.

The chapter challenges the idea that colonial rule was solely exploitative, arguing instead that the biblical influence on governance created lasting institutions of justice, administration, and law that benefited India. However, Mangalwadi also critiques the limitations and eventual decline of this influence after independence.

Argument Structure: Premises, Evidence, and Conclusion

Premise 1: Initially the British Raj was Corrupt

- **Evidence:** British rule between 1765 and 1820 was characterised by widespread corruption similar to contemporary Indian bureaucracy (p. 39).
- **Example:** British officials used the civil services to enrich themselves at the expense of Indian citizens, similar to corrupt politicians today (p. 40).

Premise 2: The Bible Transformed British Governance in India

- **Evidence:** The Evangelical movement emphasised biblical ethics in administration (p. 42–43).
- **Example:** Many ICS officers were sons of Christian pastors who were trained in Biblical integrity and prayed for moral strength in their governance roles (p. 40–41).

Premise 3: Missionary Education Promoted Ethical Civil Services

- **Evidence:** Missionary schools and Bible-based education emphasised integrity, truth, and service, producing honest administrators (p. 41–42).
- **Example:** Post-independence education, which removed biblical teachings, has led to increased corruption in India (p. 43–44).

Conclusion: The Bible Provided the Moral Foundation for Effective Governance

- The transformation of British rule in India was largely due to the

moral influence of the Bible.
- Colonialism is flawed yet the reformation of civil services under the Bible's influence created a legacy of just governance.
- The decline of biblical education has contributed to the deterioration of governance in modern India (p. 44–45).

Key Themes & Ideas

Corruption in Colonial Rule and Its Reformation (p. 39–41)

- Initially the British rule was corrupt, similar to contemporary governance.
- The Bible transformed British Indian Civil Services.

The Role of the Indian Civil Services (ICS) in Governance (p. 39–40)

- Vallabhbhai Patel's praise for the ICS as the "Steel Frame of India."
- The Bible was the key to creating a disciplined and fair administrative structure.

Evangelical Influence on British Administration (p. 42–43)

- Christian missionaries emphasised ethics, integrity, and justice in governance.
- Many ICS officers came from Christian backgrounds and upheld biblical moral values.

The Long-term Impact of Bible-based Governance (p. 43–45)

- Ethical governance structures persisted even after independence.
- The removal of biblical education has brought corruption back in governance.

Chapter 5: The Bible and Women's Liberation

Discussion and Study Questions

Understanding the Chapter

- What historical example does the author provide to illustrate the condition of women in pre-modern India? (p. 49, para. 1-3)
- How did the Bible influence missionary efforts to liberate women from slavery and oppression? (p. 50, para. 2-4)
- What biblical principle undergirds the fight against gender-based injustices like female infanticide, child marriage, and widow burning (sati)? (p. 51, para. 1-3)
- How does Mangalwadi contrast the biblical doctrine of sin with Hindu and Buddhist explanations of female subjugation? (p. 51-52, para. 4-5)
- In what ways did Christian missionaries, such as Rev. Charles Mead, help empower women in South India? (p. 50, para. 1-4)
- How does Mangalwadi use the example of Moses to argue that empowering women strengthens a nation? (p. 50, para. 5)

Analysing the Argument

- What are Mangalwadi's key arguments about the role of the Bible in women's liberation? (Refer to the Argument Structure section)
- How does Mangalwadi compare the biblical concept of gender equality to Hinduism's doctrine of karma and reincarnation? (p. 51, para. 3-5)
- How does the biblical understanding of salvation differ from the Hindu concept of self-realisation and Brahmacharya? (p. 62-63, para. 1-3)
- Did abandoning wives in the name of Sannyas or Brahmacharya empower women? (p. 50)
- What role did missionaries play in advocating for women's education and literacy in India? (p. 58-59)

Critical Thinking & Further Discussion

- How might someone argue that women's progress in India was not solely due to Christian influence? What counter-arguments does Mangalwadi provide?
- Are there any aspects of women's rights in contemporary India that still reflect challenges similar to those described in this chapter?
- How does the biblical view of gender equality align or conflict with contemporary feminist movements?
- In what ways does Mangalwadi's argument challenge mainstream historical narratives about women's rights in India?

Summary

In The Bible and Women's Liberation, Mangalwadi argues that the Bible played a foundational role in the emancipation of Indian women. He begins with the story of an eight-year-old girl rescued by Rev. Charles Mead, illustrating the deep-rooted oppression of women in pre-modern India. The chapter highlights the Bible's role in combating practices such as female infanticide, child marriage, widow burning (sati), temple prostitution and abandoning wives in pursuit of one's salvation.

Mangalwadi contrasts Hinduism's explanation of gender inequality—rooted in karma and reincarnation—with the biblical doctrine of sin. Hindu philosophy, he argues, viewed being born a woman as a consequence of bad karma, whereas the Bible saw gender oppression as a result of human sin, offering salvation and restoration through Christ. The chapter also explores how Christian missionaries advocated for legal reforms and women's education, challenging oppressive traditions.

Key Arguments

- **The Bible as the Foundation for Women's Liberation:** Mangalwadi argues that biblical teachings on human dignity, equality, and justice laid the groundwork for gender reform in India.
- **Contrast Between Biblical and Hindu Views on Women:**

While Hinduism saw female subjugation as karma's consequence, the Bible viewed it as sin's result, requiring divine redemption.
- **Missionary Advocacy for Women's Rights:** Christian missionaries like Rev. Mead and William Carey played crucial roles in abolishing harmful practices such as Sati and promoting women's literacy.
- **Biblical Influence on National Development:** Mangalwadi suggests that empowering women strengthens a nation, as seen in the biblical story of Moses and the efforts of missionaries in India.

Argument Structure: Premises, Evidence, and Conclusion

Premise 1: Pre-Biblical India Oppressed Women

Evidence:

- Women were subjected to practices such as female infanticide, Sati, child marriage, forced temple prostitution and abandonment in the name of Sannyas or Brahmacharya. (p. 51, para. 1-3)
- Hindu traditions viewed women as inferior due to bad karma, justifying their oppression. (p. 51, para. 4-5)
- Women had no legal protections or rights before the Bible influenced India's reform movements. (p. 57-58)

Premise 2: The Bible Provided a New Framework for Gender Equality

Evidence:

- The Bible teaches that men and women equally bear the image of God, offering a foundation for human dignity. (p. 50, para. 4)
- Christian missionaries actively worked to abolish slavery, Sati, women's education and respect for marriage as a life-long commitment. (p. 58-59)
- The biblical doctrine of salvation included the restoration of gender equality, unlike Hindu teachings of self-realisation and Brahmacharya. (p. 62-63)

Premise 3: The Bible Required Social and Legal Reforms
Evidence:

- The abolition of Sati and legal protections for widows were driven by missionaries' efforts. (p. 57-58)
- Education for women became a reality due to Christian obedience and advocacy. (p. 58-59)
- The Bible inspired movements for legal equality challenged the notion that oppression was divinely ordained. (p. 51-52)

Conclusion: Mangalwadi asserts that India's progress in women's rights came from the Bible. It was not an organic development within Hindu or Islamic cultures. He argues that without the Bible, these reforms would not have taken place.

Key Themes & Ideas

- **The Role of Christian Missionaries in Women's Emancipation** (p. 50, para. 2-4)

Examples: Female missionaries supported by pioneers such as Rev. Charles Mead and William Carey who devoted their lives to educate Indian women in opposition to the traditional Indian culture.

- **Biblical vs. Hindu Explanations of Gender Inequality** (p. 51, para. 3-5)

Hinduism: Women's oppression was a result of past-life karma.

The Bible: Female oppression was a result of sin; redemption through Christ restores women's lost dignity.

- **The Fight Against Social Evils Like Sati and Female Infanticide** (p. 57-58)

The Bible created the consensus against inhuman practices such as female infanticide and Sati that mythology had made "sacred."

- **Women's Education and Literacy as a Tool for Empowerment** (p. 58-59)

Educating women as a key to social progress.

164   The Bible and the Making of Modern India

- **The Bible and Gender Equality** (p. 62-63)

  The idea that true gender equality comes from recognising both men and women as bearers of God's image.

Chapter 6: The Bible and India's Green Revolution

Discussion and Study Questions

Understanding the Chapter

- What role did Norman Borlaug play in India's Green Revolution, and how did biblical principles influence his work? (p. 73, para. 1-2)
- How does Mangalwadi contrast Indian sages' philosophical pursuits with the practical application of the Bible's teachings on agriculture? (p. 73, para. 4)
- What worldview challenges did Sam Higginbottom seek to overcome in rural India? (p. 74, para. 2-3)
- How did Christian missionaries contribute to modernising Indian agriculture? (p. 75, para. 4-5)
- In what ways did biblical teachings promote human dignity in contrast to the caste-based division of labour? (p. 76, para. 1-2)

Analysing the Argument

- What key premises does Mangalwadi present to argue that the Bible laid the foundation for India's Green Revolution? (Refer to the Argument Structure section)
- How does Mangalwadi critique India's traditional approach to agriculture? (p. 73, para. 3-4)
- Does the author provide sufficient evidence that biblical influence was instrumental in India's agricultural transformation? Why or why not?
- How did Sam Higginbottom's work with farmers embody biblical

values of stewardship and service? (p. 74, para. 5)
- How does Mangalwadi differentiate the biblical vision of agriculture from traditional Hindu views of nature and land use? (p. 76, para. 3-4)

Critical Thinking & Further Discussion

- What counter arguments might be presented against Mangalwadi's claim that the Bible's influence was essential to India's Green Revolution?
- How do traditional Hindu and Buddhist views on karma and fatalism contrast with the Bible's perspective on human effort and agricultural innovation?
- What broader implications does Mangalwadi's argument have for developing nations struggling with food scarcity?
- How does the concept of stewardship in the Bible compare to the indigenous Indian approach to land and farming? (p. 77, para. 2)
- Could India's Green Revolution have happened without biblical intervention? Why or why not?

Summary

Chapter 6, The Bible and India's Green Revolution, explores how the Bible played a significant role in modernising India's agricultural system. Mangalwadi argues that India used to struggle with food shortages not due to a lack of intelligence but due to a worldview that did not emphasise practical problem-solving in agriculture and irrigation. He highlights the contributions of Christian missionaries, particularly Sam Higginbottom, irrigation engineers and agronomists such as Norman Borlaug, in transforming India's approach to food production.

Key Themes

- **India's Agricultural Stagnation and Fatalism:** Mangalwadi critiques the traditional Hindu view of agriculture as an inferior occupation reserved for the lower castes. That kept scientific progress in farming at bay. He contrasts this with the Bible's teaching that emphasised human stewardship of the land.

- **Sam Higginbottom's Contribution:** An American missionary, Higginbottom introduced scientific agriculture in Allahabad and other places, emphasising education, irrigation, and improved farming techniques.

- **The Role of the Bible in Agricultural Development:** The Bible's view of the dignity of manual work, stewardship of land and rivers provided a framework for innovation, which was absent in caste-based agrarian systems.

- **Norman Borlaug and the Green Revolution:** Mangalwadi connects Borlaug's achievements to biblical ideas of redemption from the curse on land and food production that came from sin and God's promise of abundant life, which inspired missionaries to introduce new crops and develop high-yield, disease-resistant varieties of various staple diets.

- **Comparing Worldviews:** The chapter contrasts the pessimistic Indian view that suffering is inevitable with the Bible's teaching that God wants to save sinners from the consequences of sin and enjoy abundant life.

Conclusion

Mangalwadi argues that India's Green Revolution was a product of scientific advancement that came out of a shift in worldview. The progressive worldview came from the Bible. He contends that modern India owes its success in surplus food production to the work of Christian missionaries, engineers, civil servants and agronomists who applied the Bible to address hunger and poverty.

Argument Structure: Premises, Evidence, and Conclusion

Premise 1: India's Traditional Agricultural System Was Inefficient Due to Religious Escapism and Fatalism

Evidence:

- While Buddhism saw life as inescapably suffering, traditional

Hindu thought viewed physical labour as a lower-caste occupation. That discouraged innovation and action for progress. (p. 73, para. 3-4).

- Temples and religious sites were built near rivers, but no efforts were made to develop irrigation systems for agriculture (p. 74, para. 2).
- Christian missionaries were very different from Indian sages who focused on philosophical speculation and asceticism rather than on practical science to resist hunger, poverty and suffering (p. 73, para. 4).

Premise 2: The Bible Promoted Agricultural Stewardship and Innovation

Evidence:

- The Bible teaches that human beings were created not to escape life but to take care of the earth and establish their culture upon it. (p. 75, para. 1).
- Christian missionaries like Sam Higginbottom introduced modern agricultural techniques, irrigation, and education for farmers (p. 75, para. 4-5).
- The Bible's emphasis on dignity of work, personal responsibility and labour motivated Western agronomists like Norman Borlaug to develop high-yield crops (p. 73, para. 1-2).

Premise 3: India's Green Revolution Was a Product of a Biblical Worldview

Evidence:

- Norman Borlaug, influenced by biblical ideas of service, worked to end global hunger (p. 73, para. 1).
- Sam Higginbottom's Agricultural Institute introduced farming techniques that increased food production and broke caste-based labour divisions (p. 74, para. 5).
- India's embrace of scientific agriculture was influenced by Western

education, which had biblical roots (p. 77, para. 2).

Conclusion

India's Green Revolution was made possible by a shift from an escapist fatalism to one rooted in biblical principles of the goodness of material creation, human beings as stewards of creation, not souls in bondage, creativity and service. Mangalwadi argues that the technical aspects of the agricultural revolution were scientific because its intellectual and moral foundation were shaped by the Bible's worldview.

Key Themes & Ideas

- **Hindu Escapism vs. Biblical Stewardship** (p. 73, para. 3-4): Traditional Indian beliefs discouraged active problem-solving in agriculture, whereas the Bible's teaching on salvation from sin implied deliverance from scarcity through work, stewardship and responsibility.
- **Role of Christian Missionaries in Agriculture** (p. 74, para. 5): Sam Higginbottom's emphasis on "The Gospel and the Plow" demonstrated how the Bible's worldview could change Indian agriculture.
- **Theological Basis of Agri-Revolution** (p. 75, para. 1): Scientific, technology-based agriculture was a fruit of biblical theology.
- **Food Security as a Moral Imperative** (p. 73, para. 1): The Green Revolution was not just about science but about applying ethical principles to ensure human well-being.

Chapter 7: The Bible, Not Britain, Modernised India

Discussion and Study Questions

Understanding the Chapter

- How does Mangalwadi argue that the Bible, rather than British

colonialism, was responsible for modernising India? (p. 83, para. 2-4)
- What were the key ways in which biblical teachings influenced India's legal, political, and social institutions? (p. 86, para. 1-3)
- How did British officials react to the Christian missionary influence in India? (p. 89, para. 2)
- What role did Indian reformers, inspired by biblical principles, play in shaping modern India? (p. 91, para. 3-5)
- How does Mangalwadi differentiate between colonial exploitation and biblical reform? (p. 93, para. 1-2)

Analysing the Argument

- What are the main premises of Mangalwadi's argument, and what evidence does he provide for each? (Refer to the Argument Structure section)
- How does Mangalwadi refute the claim that Britain's colonial rule was beneficial to India's progress? (p. 87, para. 2-4)
- Does Mangalwadi provide sufficient evidence to argue that the Bible was instrumental in India's modernisation? Why or why not?
- In what ways did the missionary efforts contrast with British economic policies in India? (p. 92, para. 3-5)
- What specific reforms introduced by Indian thinkers were influenced by biblical teachings? (p. 95, para. 2-3)

Critical Thinking & Further Discussion

- What counterarguments might be presented against Mangalwadi's thesis?
- Are there any other factors besides biblical influence that contributed to India's modernisation?
- How does the author's perspective challenge mainstream historical narratives about British colonialism?
- What implications does this argument have for contemporary discussions about India's colonial past?

- How does this chapter compare to previous discussions on the role of the Bible in shaping India's national identity? (p. 96, para. 3-4)

Summary

Chapter 7, The Bible, Not Britain, Modernised India, challenges the idea that British colonial rule was responsible for modernising India. Mangalwadi argues that it was not the British government, but the Bible's influence—brought by missionaries and reformers—that laid the foundations for India's transformation into a modern nation. He highlights how biblical principles of justice, equality, and moral responsibility influenced Indian social and political reforms.

The chapter contrasts the exploitative policies of the British government, such as economic extraction and administrative control, with the constructive work of Christian missionaries and Indian reformers inspired by biblical teachings. Mangalwadi emphasises that British rulers were often hostile to missionary efforts because these efforts promoted social justice and human dignity, which threatened the colonial administration's control.

Mangalwadi presents figures such as William Carey, Raja Ram Mohan Roy, and Mahatma Phule, demonstrating how their work in education, law, and social justice was deeply influenced by biblical values. He argues that concepts like individual dignity, the rule of law, and the abolition of unjust practices like Sati and caste discrimination emerged from the Bible's influence rather than British governance.

This chapter challenges conventional historical narratives that credit British colonialism with India's modernisation. Instead, Mangalwadi contends that biblical reformers, both foreign and Indian, played the key role in transforming India's educational, legal, and social institutions.

Argument Structure: Premises, Evidence, and Conclusion

Premise 1: British Colonial Rule Was Primarily Exploitative Evidence:

- British policies prioritised economic extraction rather than social development (p. 83, para. 2-4).

- The British administration often opposed missionary efforts that promoted social reforms (p. 86, para. 1-3).
- Colonial policies reinforced caste divisions rather than dismantling them (p. 87, para. 2-4).

Premise 2: The Bible Introduced the Foundations of Modern Indian Society Evidence:

- Missionaries introduced vernacular education, which empowered the lower castes (p. 89, para. 2-3).
- Biblical teachings on justice and equality inspired key Indian reformers such as Raja Ram Mohan Roy and Pandita Ramabai (p. 91, para. 3-5).
- Christian values helped frame India's emerging constitutional and legal structures (p. 93, para. 1-2).

Premise 3: India's Social and Political Progress Stemmed from Biblical Influence Evidence:

- The idea of universal education, promoted by missionaries, contrasted with the British model of elite education (p. 94, para. 3-4).
- Biblical principles challenged Hindu orthodoxy on issues such as widow remarriage and female education (p. 95, para. 2-3).
- The rule of law and modern democratic values in India were shaped by the biblical worldview, not colonial rule (p. 96, para. 3-4).

Conclusion: India's modernisation was driven not by British colonial rule but by the influence of biblical principles, as introduced by missionaries and adopted by Indian reformers. The Bible's emphasis on justice, education, and human dignity provided the intellectual and moral foundation for India's transformation into a modern nation. This challenges the narrative that colonial rule was the primary driver of progress in India.

Key Themes & Ideas

Colonial Exploitation vs. Biblical Reform (p. 83, para. 2-4)
- British rule prioritised economic gain over social welfare.
- Missionary efforts, in contrast, focused on uplifting marginalised communities.

Biblical Influence on Indian Social Reformers (p. 91, para. 3-5)
- Reformers such as William Carey, Raja Ram Mohan Roy, and Mahatma Phule were influenced by biblical teachings.
- The Bible introduced concepts of justice, human dignity, and gender equality to India's reform movements.

The Bible's Role in Framing India's Legal and Political Systems (p. 93, para. 1-2)
- The rule of law, constitutional governance, and individual rights in India were inspired by biblical principles.
- The Westminster model, adopted in India, reflects biblical values of self-governance and moral responsibility.

Missionary Education vs. British Colonial Education (p. 94, para. 3-4)
- Missionaries promoted universal education in vernacular languages, empowering lower castes.
- The British model of education was elitist, designed to serve the colonial administration.

Chapter 8: The Bible and India's Independence

Discussion and Study Questions

Understanding the Chapter

- How does Vishal Mangalwadi challenge the conventional story of

India's independence? (p. 103–104)
- What role did Thomas Babington Macaulay play in shaping British policies towards India's governance? (p. 104)
- How did Charles Trevelyan argue that Christian education should prepare Indians for self-rule? (p. 104–105)
- What was the British Parliament's perspective on India's independence as early as 1833? (p. 104)
- How does Mangalwadi compare the influence of the Bible on India's freedom movement during British rule to the absence of independence movements during the seven centuries of Muslim rule in Delhi? (p. 103–104)
- How does the author explain the British decision to grant independence without a war? (p. 103–104)
- What role did the Bible play in shaping the idea of national sovereignty that eventually led to India's independence? (p. 105–106)
- How does Mangalwadi contrast European imperialism with the Bible's concept of nationhood? (p. 106–107)

Analysing the Argument

- What are the key premises of Mangalwadi's argument, and what evidence does he provide for each? (Refer to the Argument Structure section)
- Does Mangalwadi provide sufficient historical evidence to argue that biblical principles played the decisive role in India's independence? Why or why not?
- How does the author's argument challenge the mainstream narrative of India's independence being mainly a result of Mahatma Gandhi's efforts? (p. 103–104)
- What does Mangalwadi mean when he states that the "Bible was the force that liberated India"? (p. 103)

Critical Thinking & Further Discussion

- What counter arguments might be presented against Mangalwadi's thesis?
- How does the idea that Britain saw India's independence as a "moral duty to God" align or conflict with other historical accounts?
- What was the role of the Protestant Reformation and the Peace of Westphalia in shaping modern concepts of nationhood as discussed by Mangalwadi? (p. 106–107)
- How does the author contrast European imperialism with Hindu concepts like "Ashwamedh Yajna"? (p. 107)

Summary

Chapter 8, The Bible and India's Independence, challenges the popular narrative that India's freedom was primarily achieved through the efforts of Mahatma Gandhi and the Indian National Congress. Vishal Mangalwadi argues that the foundations for India's independence were laid much earlier—by the Bible that transformed European imperialism in favour of Jewish vision of sovereign nations. The Indian National Congress was born because of the Bible's worldview.

The chapter recounts the history of British colonial rule from the East India Company's dominance after the battles of Plassey (1757) and Buxar (1764) to the transfer of power to the British Crown following the 1857 revolt. While the Quit India Movement (1942) and Gandhi's non-violent resistance are often cited as the primary reasons for India's independence, Mangalwadi questions why Britain, which suppressed revolts and won two World Wars, decided to withdraw peacefully.

Mangalwadi attributes India's independence to the Bible's influence on British governance. He highlights Thomas Babington Macaulay's advocacy in 1833 that India should be governed in a way to prepare it for self-rule. Macaulay's brother-in-law, Charles Trevelyan, an evangelical civil servant, further emphasised that Christian education should not merely train Indians for colonial administration but should prepare them to govern India independently. These ideas, grounded in the Bible's vision of justice and national sovereignty, eventually led to India's freedom.

The chapter also explores how biblical principles helped shape the global shift away from imperialism. The Peace of Westphalia (1648), which ended the Thirty Years' War, introduced the Bible's idea of nationhood as an alternative to empire. This concept went on to influence movements like the American Revolution (1775–1783) and ultimately contributed to India's independence.

Mangalwadi critiques Hinduism's historical association with imperialistic expansion, citing the Ashwamedh Yajna (Horse Sacrifice) as an example of religious justification for conquest. He argues that the Bible, rather than indigenous traditions, played the key role in shaping the ethical and political framework that enabled India to gain sovereignty.

Argument Structure: Premises, Evidence, and Conclusion

Premise 1: The British Decision to Grant India Independence Was Rooted in the Bible's Moral Worldview

Evidence:

- As early as 1833, the British Parliament debated India's future self-rule as Britain's moral duty to God. (p. 104)
- Macaulay argued that British governance in India should prepare the nation for independence. (p. 104)
- Charles Trevelyan advocated for Christian education to train future Indian leaders. (p. 104–105)
- The British withdrawal in 1947 happened despite their military capability to maintain control. (p. 103)

Premise 2: The Bible Inspired the Concept of National Sovereignty that Led to Independence
Evidence:

- The Peace of Westphalia (1648) introduced the biblical/Jewish concept of nation-states, rejecting imperialism. (p. 106–107)
- Protestant Reformation promoted the idea of self-governance under God. (p. 106–107)

- The American Revolution and subsequent independence movements were influenced by biblical principles of nationhood, freedom, and governance. (p. 106)

Premise 3: Hinduism Did Not Provide a Framework for National Liberation

Evidence:

- India remained under foreign rule for centuries without producing a leader like Gandhi. (p. 103–104)
- Hinduism's caste-based and fatalistic worldview hindered the development of national consciousness. (p. 104)
- The Ashwamedh Yajna promoted imperial expansion rather than national sovereignty. (p. 107)

Conclusion: India's independence was not merely the result of political movements but was deeply influenced by biblical teachings on justice, governance, and nationhood. While figures like Gandhi played a role, the foundational ideas that led to India's self-rule were shaped by Christian education and biblical morality introduced by British reformers and missionaries.

Key Themes & Ideas

Biblical Influence on British Colonial Policy (p. 104)
- Macaulay and Trevelyan's advocacy for India's self-rule
- Christian education as a tool for preparing future Indian leaders

The Bible's Role in Shaping the Modern Concept of Nationhood (p. 106–107)
- The Peace of Westphalia and the rejection of empire-based governance
- The role of biblical principles in the American and Indian independence movements

Critique of Hinduism's Historical Governance Models (p. 103–104)

- The lack of a nationalist movement before or during the Muslim era
- The caste system as a hindrance to national unity

Comparison Between Biblical and Hindu Views on Sovereignty (p. 107)

- The biblical idea of self-governing nations versus Hindu imperial rituals like the Ashwamedh Yajna

Chapter 9: The Bible and the Soul of Modern India

Discussion and Study Questions

Understanding the Chapter

- How does Mangalwadi argue that the Bible played a crucial role in shaping modern India's values and institutions? (p. 117, para. 2–4)
- What are the key differences between India's historical religious outlook and the biblical vision of governance and social justice? (p. 119, para. 3)
- How did biblical principles influence key social reformers in India, including those who were not Christians? (p. 120, para. 5–6)
- What role did missionaries and Bible translators play in shaping India's intellectual landscape? (p. 122, para. 1)
- Why does Mangalwadi claim that modern India's sense of national identity is rooted in the Bible rather than indigenous traditions? (p. 124, para. 2)

Analysing the Argument

- What evidence does Mangalwadi provide to support the claim that the Bible led India towards a republican/democratic government? (p. 125, para. 3)
- How does the author differentiate between the impact of the Bible

and British colonial rule on India's modernisation? (p. 127, para. 4)
- What were some of the Bible-inspired reforms that influenced India's independence movement? (p. 129, para. 3)
- Does Mangalwadi provide sufficient historical evidence to demonstrate that the Bible was central to India's moral and legal transformation? Why or why not? (p. 131, para. 1)

Critical Thinking & Further Discussion

- What counter arguments could be made against Mangalwadi's claim that India's modern values were shaped primarily by the Bible?
- How did non-biblical influences (e.g., Hindu-Buddhist philosophy or Islamic governance,) compared to the Bible's influences, including through Western Enlightenment, shape modern India?
- In what ways does the argument challenge mainstream historical narratives about India's progress?
- What would be the implications of rejecting the Bible's role in shaping India's identity?

Summary

Chapter 9, The Bible and the Soul of Modern India, argues that biblical principles were instrumental in shaping India's modern identity, influencing its governance, education, and social reforms. Mangalwadi posits that India's transition into a democratic nation was not merely a byproduct of British rule but rather a result of biblical principles intentionally introduced through missionaries, reformers, and biblical education.

The chapter explores how the Bible's emphasis on human dignity, justice, and equality challenged the pessimistic and escapist caste-based structures historically dominant in Indian society. Mangalwadi discusses the role of missionaries such as William Carey, who began transforming oral dialects into literary languages through Bible translations, thereby fostering literacy and social consciousness among marginalised communities.

A significant argument in the chapter is that although leaders such as Raja Ram Mohan Roy, Mahatma Gandhi, and B.R. Ambedkar did not become overtly Christian, they were deeply influenced by the Bible in their fight against social evils like widow-burning (sati), caste discrimination, untouchability, and colonialism. The chapter contrasts this with the hierarchical governance of Hindu and Mughal traditions, arguing that the Bible provided a unifying moral and legal foundation for modern India.

Mangalwadi also critiques contemporary efforts to downplay the Bible's influence on Indian history. He argues that ignoring the Bible's role in shaping the nation erases an essential part of its intellectual and moral heritage and weakens India's future. The chapter concludes by asserting that the Bible remains central to India's moral fabric, even as contemporary society moves away from its foundational values.

Argument Structure: Premises, Evidence, and Conclusion

Premise 1: The Bible Shaped India's National Identity Evidence:

- India's pre-colonial governance was fragmented into caste-based hierarchies with no unified national vision (p. 117, para. 2–4).
- The idea of a democratic nation-state emerged from biblical influences rather than indigenous traditions (p. 119, para. 5–6).

Premise 2: Biblical Teachings Inspired Social Reforms Evidence:

- Reformers such as Raja Ram Mohan Roy, Jyotirao Phule, and Dr. Ambedkar fought against caste oppression, drawing inspiration from biblical notions of human dignity (p. 120, para. 3).
- Translation of the Bible into vernacular languages was foundational in spreading literacy and socio-political awareness (p. 122, para. 1).

Premise 3: The Bible Provided the Moral Framework for Gov-

ernance Evidence:

- British missionaries introduced education systems based on biblical principles, promoting freedom, equality, human rights, and justice (p. 125, para. 4).
- India's constitution, educational, democratic, economic, and legal institutions are based on biblical teachings and cannot be sustained without the Bible (p. 127, para. 3).

Conclusion: India's modern constitutional identity, democracy, and legal systems came from the Bible. They are not a natural evolution of indigenous traditions. The chapter challenges the narrative that India's progress was solely a result of Hindu (or Mughal) governance. It argues that the Bible shaped modern India's soul.

Key Themes & Ideas

- **Biblical Influence on National Identity:** The role of Christian politicians, missionaries, and reformers in shaping India's moral and intellectual foundation (p. 117).
- **Social Reform Movements:** The impact of biblical teachings on movements against caste discrimination, widow-burning, and untouchability (p. 120).
- **Democracy and Governance:** How biblical principles influenced India's legal and political systems (p. 125).
- **Education and Literacy:** The role of Bible translations in developing modern Indian languages and education (p. 122).
- **Contrast with Indigenous Traditions:** How the Bible's teachings on justice and equality differ from the caste system and Mughal governance (p. 127).

Chapter 10: The Bible and India's Future

Discussion and Study Questions

Understanding the Chapter

- How does Mangalwadi argue that India's future depends on embracing biblical truth? (p. 127, para. 1)
- What role does the Bible play in transforming the poor and marginalised communities in India? (p. 127, para. 3-5)
- What challenges does Mangalwadi identify within the Indian Church, and how does he suggest they can be overcome? (p. 127, para. 6)
- How does the example of a student-led slum school illustrate the potential for grassroot transformation in India? (p. 128, para. 1-4)
- In what ways does the biblical concept of repentance shape Mangalwadi's vision for India's future? (p. 129, para. 2-3)

Analysing the Argument

- What key premises does Mangalwadi use to argue that biblical principles are essential for India's national development? (Refer to Argument Structure section)
- How does Mangalwadi contrast the transformation seen in biblical societies with the stagnation found in non-biblical cultures? (p. 130, para. 2-3)
- What implications does the slum education initiative have for India's approach to poverty alleviation? (p. 131, para. 1-2)
- How does Mangalwadi's vision challenge other narratives about India's development? (p. 131, para. 4-5)
- What alternative explanations might be given for India's socio-economic challenges, and how does Mangalwadi respond to them? (p. 132, para. 1)

Critical Thinking & Further Discussion

- How does Mangalwadi's view align with or differ from other perspectives on India's national development?
- Are there any examples from Indian history where biblical principles led to positive social change?
- What counter arguments could be made against Mangalwadi's assertion that the Bible is essential for India's transformation?
- How do biblical principles compare with other religious or philosophical approaches to governance and social reform in India?
- In what ways does education play a role in shaping a nation's moral and ethical foundation?

Summary

Chapter 10, The Bible and India's Future, presents Mangalwadi's vision for India's national transformation through Bible-based education. He argues that India has the potential to become one of the world's greatest nations by repenting of its sins and embracing truth. However, he notes that a portion of the Indian Church has been influenced by the prevailing culture of corruption, yet a new, post-colonial Church is emerging, particularly among the marginalised poor.

Mangalwadi illustrates his argument with the story of a young student teaching children in a slum. This initiative, which started with a small group, grew into a significant educational movement supported by technological advancements. The story highlights how biblical influence fosters private initiative, education and economic change based on compassion and personal responsibility.

According to Mangalwadi, India's progress has been hindered by a worldview that relies on government and tolerates injustice and fatalism. He contrasts this with the Bible's power to transform individuals, which led to intellectual, moral and economic advancements in the West. He asserts that true national renewal requires a spiritual foundation grounded in biblical truth, which can uplift even the most underprivileged members of society.

Ultimately, the chapter argues that India's future depends on a return to the Bible, which provides the ethical and intellectual framework necessary for sustained national development.

Argument Structure: Premises, Evidence, and Conclusion

Premise 1: India Needs a Moral and Spiritual Revival Evidence:

- A culture of corruption has weakened India's progress, and the Bible provides an alternative ethical foundation (p. 127, para. 3-4).
- True wealth of a nation lies hidden in the soul of its people. Therefore, sustainable transformation begins at the grassroots level, as seen in the slum education initiative (p. 128, para. 2-3).
- Repentance and truth are central to building a just and prosperous society (p. 129, para. 1).

Premise 2: Biblical Principles Have Proven Transformative in Other Societies Evidence:

- Western nations that embraced biblical values experienced social and economic progress (p. 130, para. 1-2).
- Education and literacy, driven by biblical influence, have historically played a crucial role in national development (p. 131, para. 1).
- Biblical principles challenge corruption inducing worldviews which cause poverty and stagnation in non-biblical societies (p. 131, para. 3).

Premise 3: The Emerging Church in India Can Lead the Nation's Transformation Evidence:

- A new movement within the Indian Church is focused on social reform and moral integrity (p. 127, para. 6).
- Persecution has refined and strengthened the faith of the marginalised, making them key agents of change (p. 128, para. 4).
- The slum education initiative demonstrates the potential for faith-based transformation in practical ways (p. 129, para. 3-4).

Conclusion: India can become a great nation by embracing biblical truth and moral reform. Without these principles, corruption, poverty, and social division will grow. India can experience a cultural and economic revival through obedience to biblical revelation. Reforming education that the Bible fosters is necessary for the upliftment of all. (p. 132, para. 2)

Key Themes & Ideas

The Bible's Role in National Development (p. 127, para. 2)
- The Bible provides a moral framework necessary for justice and upliftment of all.

Grassroots Transformation Through Education (p. 128, para. 1-3)
- God desires upliftment of the lowliest. This is facilitated by changing the minds of those who control a society's power-centers.

Challenges Within the Indian Church (p. 127, para. 6)
- Some churches have internalised corruption that rules India, but a new movement is emerging.

Biblical Repentance and Renewal (p. 129, para. 1-2)
- National change requires change of mind and spiritual repentance.

Historical Examples of Biblical Influence (p. 130, para. 1-2)
- Western nations experienced growth through biblical ethics and education.

The Impact of Fatalism vs. Biblical Hope (p. 131, para. 3)
- Fatalism leads to stagnation, while biblical hope inspires progress.

Further Reading & Bibliography References

1. Mangalwadi, Vishal
- The Bible and the Making of Modern India
- The Book That Made Your World; How The Bible Created the Soul of Western Civilisation
- India: The Grand Experiment
- Missionary Conspiracy: Letters to a Postmodern Hindu
- This Book Changed Everything: The Bible's Amazing Impact on Our World
- The Father of Modern India: William Carey
- Moving Backward Castes Forward

2. Additional References
- Samson, Steven Alan. Vishal Mangalwadi: The Book That Made Your World Study Guide (2011-2012)
- Carey, William. A Grammar of the Bengali Language
- Prinsep, James. Essays on Indian Antiquities
- Grant, Charles. Observations on the State of Society Among the Asiatic Subjects of Great Britain
- Premchand. Godaan (A novel depicting Indian peasant life and fatalism)
- Wilberforce, William. A Practical View of Christianity
- Drucker, Peter. Management: Tasks, Responsibilities, Practices (on ICS as a model of governance)
- Bradley, Ian. A Call to Seriousness: The Evangelical Impact on British Society
- Landes, David. The Wealth and Poverty of Nations
- Weber, Max. The Protestant Ethic and the Spirit of Capitalism
- Popper, Karl. The Logic of Scientific Discovery
- Augustine, St. Confessions
- Boethius. The Consolation of Philosophy
- Babu Verghese. Let There Be India: Impact of the Bible on Nation Building

Other Books by Vishal Mangalwadi

1. *The World of Gurus* - Vikas Publishing House (Delhi, 1977)

2. *Truth and Social Reform* - Nivedit Good Books (New Delhi, 1985) and Hodder & Stoughton (London, UK, 1989)

3. *The Father of Modern India: William Carey*, Sought After Media (Clovis, CA 2024) earlier published as *William Carey: A Tribute by an Indian Woman* (With Ruth Mangalwadi), Nivedit Good Books (New Delhi, 1992). Expanded edits of this book were subsequently published under various titles in the UK, S. Korea, China, USA, Mexico, Brazil, etc.

4. *In Search of Self: Beyond the New Age* (Hodder & Stoughton London, 1991) and IVP (Downer's Grove, IL, 1992) published as When The New Age Gets Old: Looking For a Greater Spirituality

5. *What Liberates A Woman: The Story of Pandita Ramabai—A Builder of Modern India* (Main author - Nicol MacNicol, Introduction by Vishal Mangalwadi) - Nivedit Good Books, (New Delhi, 1996)

6. *Dear Rajan: Letters to a New Believer* GLS (Bombay, 1995)

7. *Missionary Conspiracy: Letters to a Postmodern Hindu* - Nivedit Good Books (Mussoorie, 1996)

8. *India: The Grand Experiment* - Pippa Rann Books, (UK 1997)

9. *Corruption vs. True Spirituality* (Incorporating True Spirituality by Francis Schaefer) - Nivedit Good Books (Mussoorie, 1998)

10. *Why Must You Convert?* - Nivedit Good Books, (Mussoorie, 1999)

11. *The Bible in India* (Wisdom from India Series) - Nivedit Good Books (Mussoorie, 2000)

12. *Astrology* (Wisdom from India Series) - Nivedit Good Books, (Mussoorie, 2000)

13. *Fascism: Modern and Postmodern* (Main author - Gene Edward Veith) - Nivedit Good Books (Mussoorie, 2000)

14. *The Quest For Freedom & Dignity: Caste, Conversion & Cultural Revolution* - GLS Publishing, (Bombay, 2001)

15. *Spirituality of Hate: A Futuristic Perspective on Indo-Pakistan Conflict* - Horizon Printers & Publishers, (Delhi, 2002)

16. *Burnt Alive: The Stains and the God They Loved* (with Babu Verghese, Vijay Martis and others) - GLS Publishing, (Bombay, 2006)

17. *Truth and Transformation: A Manifesto for Ailing Nations* - YWAM Publishing, (Seattle, 2009)

18. *Obama, The Presidency and the Bible* (Pasadena, 2008)

19. *The Book That Made Your World: How the Bible Created the Soul of Western Civilisation* - Thomas Nelson Inc. (Nashville, 2011)

20. *Why Are We Backward? :Roots, Myths and True Hope for Development* - Forward Press, (New Delhi, 2013). Now being published as *Moving Backward Castes Forward* - Sought After Media, 2024

21. *The Gospel and the Plough* (Main author - Sam Higginbottom) - Nivedit Good Books, (Mussoorie, 2016)

22. *This Book Changed Everything: The Bible's Amazing Impact on Our World* - Sought After Media (Pasadena, 2019)

23. *Don't Let Schooling Stand In The Way of Education* (Main author - Darrow L. Miller) - Credo House Publishers, 2021

24. *The Third Education Revolution: From Home School to Church College* (Editor and Co-author) - Sought After Media, (Pasadena, 2021)

25. *Conversion: The Revolution India Needs* - Sought After Media, (Clovis, 2023)

26. *Healing the Open Wounds of Islam* (An abridged German edition has been published. The English language edition is in the pipeline)

27. *GIRL: Abort or Empower Her* (co-author, Ruth Mangalwadi) Sought After Media (Clovis, 2023)

Acknowledgements

This book is only an appetiser for a multi-volume series, tentatively called "How The Bible Created Modern India." That study undertaken by about 40 authors has been coordinated by Mr. Prasanth David under the banner of India Research 75. For this introductory volume, I have borrowed a few segments of the research done by Dr. Mercia Justin, Dr. Blesson Paul, Mr. David Samuelson, Prof. Ashish Alexander and Dr. Babu Verghese. This book is meant to wet your appetite for the full chapters by these researchers, to be published in the forthcoming volumes.

Completing a book like this in less than a month would have been impossible without Ms. Oyila Veer bearing the burden for this project. Some day I hope to meet this incredible young woman who collected my thoughts from different places to compile the first draft.

The idea that this book should be published to celebrate my 75th birthday came from Andrew Jerome. Early versions of a few of these chapters were filmed by Triaze.com. Others were scripted at Dr. Rahil Patel's request in the Fall of 2023 for the Oxford Center for Christian Apologetics.

David Linden and Prof. Ashish Alexander volunteered their time and talent to edit the first edition of the book. The revised edition is edited by Mr. Martin Chekuri and Dr. Anandit Mu. The study guide is prepared by Mr. George Anthony Paul. The original cover was designed by Iver Pandian and refined by Praneeth Franklin in this version.

I am very grateful to Dr. Richard Howell for contributing the Foreword and to Advocate Priya Aristotle and team for planning the release and distribution.

www.ingramcontent.com/pod-product-compliance
Lightning Source LLC
LaVergne TN
LVHW061610070526
838199LV00078B/7236